Dear Nancy,

Other books in the growing Faithgirlz!™ library

The Faithgirlz! Bible
My Faithgirlz! Journal

Nonfiction

Beauty Lab, Body Talk, Girl Politics, and
Everybody Tells Me to Be Myself but I Don''t Know Who I Am

Other books by Nancy Rue

The Sophie Series

Sophie's World (Book One)

Sophie's Secret (Book Two)

Sophie and the Scoundrels
(Book Three)

Sophie's Irish Showdown (Book Four)

Sophie's First Dance? (Book Five)

Sophie's Stormy Summer (Book Six)

Sophie Breaks the Code (Book Seven)

Sophie Tracks a Thief (Book Eight)

Sophie Flakes Out (Book Nine)

Sophie Loves Jimmy (Book Ten)

Sophie Loses the Lead (Book Eleven)

Sophie's Encore (Book Twelve)

Lily Series

Here's Lily! (Book One)

Lily Robbins, M.D. (Book Two)

Lily and the Creep (Book Three)

Lily's Ultimate Party (Book Four)

Ask Lily (Book Five)

Lily the Rebel (Book Six)

Lights, Action, Lily! (Book Seven)

Lily Rules! (Book Eight)

Rough & Rugged Lily (Book Nine)

Lily Speaks! (Book Ten)

Horse Crazy Lily (Book Eleven)

Lily's Church Camp Adventure
(Book Twelve)

Lily's in London?! (Book Thirteen)

Lily's Passport to Paris
(Book Fourteen)

Check out www.faithgirlz.com

Dear Nancy,

answers to letters from girls like you

Nancy Rue

Compiled by Marijean S. Rue

ZONDERVAN.com/
AUTHORTRACKER
follow your favorite authors

www.zonderkidz.com

Dear Nancy

Copyright © 2008 by Nancy Rue

Requests for information should be addressed to:
Zonderkidz, *Grand Rapids, Michigan* 49530

Library of Congress Cataloging-in-Publication Data

Rue, Nancy N.
    Dear Nancy : answers to letters from girls like you / by Nancy Rue ; compiled by
Marijean S. Rue.
       p. cm.— (Faithgirlz)
     ISBN 978-0-310-71496-5 (softcover)
     1. Rue, Nancy N.—Juvenile literature. 2. Authors, American— 20th century—
Correspondence—Juvenile literature. 3. Rue, Nancy N. Sophie series—Miscellanea—Juvenile literature. 4. Rue, Nancy N. Lily series—Miscellanea—Juvenile
literature. 5. Girls—Miscellanea—Juvenile literature. 6. Friendship—
Miscellanea—Juvenile literature. 7. Adolescence—Miscellanea—Juvenile literature.
8. Girls—Family relationships—Miscellanea—Juvenile literature. 9. Girls—Religious
life—Miscellanea—Juvenile literature. I. Rue, Marijean. II. Title.
PS3568.U3595Z48 2008

813'.54—dc22   2008017710

All Scripture quotations, unless otherwise indicated, are taken from the HOLY BIBLE, NEW
INTERNATIONAL VERSION®. NIV®. Copyright © 1973, 1978, 1984 by International Bible Society. Used by permission of Zondervan. All rights reserved.

Scripture quotations from *THE MESSAGE*. Copyright © by Eugene H. Peterson 1993, 1994,
1995, 1996, 2000, 2001, 2002. Used by permission of NavPress Publishing Group.

Internet addresses (websites, blogs, etc.) and telephone numbers printed in this book
are offered as a resource to you. These are not intended in any way to be or imply an
endorsement on the part of Zondervan, nor do we vouch for the content of these sites and
numbers for the life of this book.

Published in association with the literary agency of Alive Communications, Inc., 7680 God-
dard Street Suite 200, Colorado Springs, CO 80920. www.alivecommunications.com

Art direction: Merit Alderink
Interior design: Melissa Elenbaas

Printed in the United States of America

08 09 10 11 12 • 25 24 23 22 21 20 19 18 17 16 15 14 13 12 11 10 9 8 7 6 5 4 3 2

So we fix our eyes not on what is seen, but on what is unseen. For what is seen is temporary, but what is unseen is eternal.

—2 Corinthians 4:18

Table of Contents

Introduction
You've Got Mail

For a long time, there was this big laundry basket in the corner of my office. Sometimes, when I was feeling guilty, I would put it inside the closet or cover it with an afghan. Then, one day, I realized it had multiplied—like some kind of amoeba—and suddenly there were *two* laundry baskets to be shuffled around or hidden under afghans. And when those little storage baskets lined with fabric came on the market, some of them started appearing in my office as well. I was running out of afghans.

Each of these baskets was filled to overflowing with fan mail. Some came in big batches from one of my publishers, and some showed up in my P.O. Box. Some made their way to my home address, usually from people who lived in Tennessee and had managed to look me up. There were letters on that grayish paper with the big lines written in shaky, blocky handwriting, and letters on lovely stationery written in I-just-learned-how cursive. There were pictures of readers, some actual photographs, and some self-portraits in crayon, pen, marker, and even sticker collages. There were long descriptions of the plights of nine-year-old girls, short missives to the tune of "I like your books; they are good," and pleas for just *one more* installment in this or that series. There were also plenty of suggestions about my writing—what character should do what, how I should have ended such-and-such book, where I'd gone terribly, horribly wrong with this or that story, and, of course, what I should write next.

I love them all. I love mail!

I absolutely pore over the letters my readers send me. I love to read them. It's as though you're all right there with me, as though I can see your beautiful young faces and hear your high-pitched kid voices telling me everything I always wanted to hear about my writing. I love to write for kids, because you're so generous, and you state things in the plainest terms: "I like this." "This is great." "I LLL-LOOOOVVVVEEEE your books!!!" If everyone had that kind of encouragement, we'd all be cranking out novels, let me tell you!

And I really do mean to answer every letter. Otherwise, why would I keep them? If I didn't intend to write back, I'd just read them and say, "That's nice. What's for lunch?" and toss them, right? But I *did* keep them. I kept them for *years*. I kept them until my daughter grew up and got a master's degree and then came to work for me and said, "Mother! These poor kids! What is the matter with you?"

My daughter and I have a very special relationship, as I'm sure you can tell.

Anyway, Marijean (that's my daughter) was a great assistant, and she made sure that no note went unanswered. She spent an entire summer going through the baskets, organizing the letters into piles according to subject, and then sending a general apology letter that many of you received. Then, when a new letter came in, Marijean read it out loud to me as I was writing the next Sophie or Faithgirlz book and said, "Shall we tell him/her _____?" and I would say, "I love that!" She typed it, and I signed it, and it ACTUALLY went into the mail (with a stamp and everything).

After doing this for a while, Marijean noticed that a lot of kids ask the same questions. And when I travel and teach workshops, I notice that kids always ask one or all of the following questions:

✎ Is it fun to be a writer?
✎ Is it hard to be a writer?
✎ How did you become a writer?

There also seems to be a general interest in my childhood, the type of food I like to eat, whether I have pets, kids, or a husband, and my favorite Scripture verse.

When I really got into writing for tween girls about the hard stuff you have to face sometimes, I started getting mail that had a lot of questions of a different kind — hard questions, questions that you wish you had someone in your life you could ask, but it's just too weird to try and get that information from your mom, your youth pastor, or your teacher. And it was one thing when I was letting the "You're super-duper great!" letters slide without so much as a post-card, but girls needed to *know* the answers to the hard questions.

Finally, it hit me like my black lab when he hadn't seen me for a week. If I'm not good at writing letters, but I'm good at writing books, then I should *answer* the letters *with a book.*

Duh.

We found all the really good questions and whipped up what you now hold in your hot little hands. In this book you should find:

✎ all the information about me you could possibly desire;
✎ the must-knows about those astonishing, amazing girls, Sophie and Lily;
✎ all kinds of tips and tricks for being a writer;
✎ stuff you did NOT want to ask your school nurse about your body;

- ✎ tricky, sticky friend situations (And what *about* those creatures called boys?);
- ✎ things you really don't think you can talk to your family about;
- ✎ ways to be your absolutely true self;
- ✎ AND those really, really hard-core questions girls write to me about.

I still want to get your letters, and I want to answer them. But think of this book as your own personal note straight from the desk of Nancy Rue—whatever *you* think that desk looks like—and know that even if you never get an actual, stamped, addressed envelope from me, you—because you're my wonderful, excited, thoughtful, smart, loyal reader—are always in my heart.

Or my laundry basket.

chapter one

Here's Nancy's World!
Everything You've Ever Asked about Nancy Rue

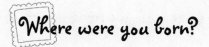 **Where were you born?**

I was born in Riverside, New Jersey, which is across the river from Philadelphia — home of Philly cheesesteaks and Benjamin Franklin (he was long gone by the time I came along). I only lived there until I was four, and then my mom, dad, brother and sister, and I moved to Jacksonville, Florida. Back then, Florida was still pretty much an unsettled swamp, full of freaky bugs and really poisonous snakes. One day, some men asked if they could go into our backyard and catch the ALLIGATOR that was living there — I am so not kidding!

Every summer we drove up the Eastern Seaboard to visit family in New Jersey for several weeks. I couldn't wait to get there and eat big, soft pretzels (there were none in Florida) and go to the Jersey seashore, where I loved the boardwalks and the sun didn't instantly turn me into an intensive-care burn victim. So I still feel like I have roots in the tri-state area, as it's known.

How old are you?

I was born in 1951, so this year, in July, I turned 57. Doesn't that sound old? I used to think so, but I don't feel old at all. Inside, sometimes I'm eight—when I get excited about the next film from Pixar—and sometimes I'm twelve—when friends are coming for an overnight visit. Hello! Sleepover! I think we can be any age that we are in our hearts. Have you ever met those kids who are just not kids, but little CEOs in pre-teen bodies? Most of the time I like being the me I am today, with the happy wrinkles around my eyes and the funky brown spots on my hands that remind me of my mom.

What made you want to start writing?

What made me want to start writing was reading. I was a big-time reader from the time I was about four. I positively devoured books, and from about the age of seven, that was especially true of mysteries. I read all the Trixie Belden, Bobbsey Twins, and Cherry Ames books I could find. But my favorite was Nancy Drew. I wanted to BE

"We're taking you to an Eagles game," Mom said. "Sunday. In Philly."

She looked at Lily. "I know this isn't a thrill for you, but I thought you'd have fun watching the cheerleaders and the halftime show. You never see those things on TV. If all else fails, they have great hot dogs."

(from *Lily the Rebel*)

her — she was so awesome. She didn't go to school or work. She had a housekeeper and the two coolest friends ever. She wore amazing clothes, had thick, gorgeous blonde hair, and tooled around in a little blue roadster solving all the crimes her lawyer father was too lame to figure out. I didn't even know what a roadster was, but I wanted one badly. There were only so many Nancy Drew books, so I read them over and over until I practically had them memorized. And then, one day, it just occurred to me that I could write stories too.

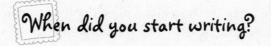

When did you start writing?

When I was ten, I had just finished reading a Nancy Drew book for, like, the fourth time (or maybe 44th), and I suddenly thought, *I could write something like this!* I think I had gotten to the point where I was so saturated — like, in it up to my eyebrows — with the reading that I needed to start getting some words out of my head, or it was going to explode. So I dragged out my sister's typewriter and began my first novel. It was called, "The Mystery of Eleanor Village." (Catchy, huh?) Eleanor Village was a little resort where my family had spent a long weekend. The whole time, all I could think of was what a cool place it would be for solving a crime, and I came up with this whole story in my head. It was going to blow Nancy Drew right out of her roadster.

I cranked out a couple of pages and then took them, full of pride, to my dad, who was just my absolute favorite person in the world and who obviously knew everything. He read it and smiled, and then he started helpfully pointing out where I could make some changes.

Um, excuse me ... CHANGES!??!?! This was my masterpiece!!!!!!!

He meant well, but I was a really, REALLY sensitive child, and I was completely crushed. I put everything away and didn't write anything more than spelling words until, well, after college.

Of course I wrote things like papers and essays—the stuff that got me through college with my degree in English and my teacher's certificate. I got married, moved from Florida to Virginia with my new husband, and started teaching English at Booker T. Washington High School. It was 1973, and this school in downtown Norfolk, Virginia, was filled with African American students who'd lived in that neighborhood all their lives and a small group of white students who were being bused in to satisfy the requirements of desegregation—that is, so there would be an even number of black kids and white kids. It was pretty tense because kids from different races weren't used to going to school together. When people are faced with a new situation, they get scared and some of them act out. I saw a lot of fights in the cafeteria. I was given English classes to teach where some of the kids were still having a hard time with reading. On the first day of class, I looked out at a sea of afro hairdos framing I-dare-you faces and then opened the textbook. The first writing assignment was "Write an essay about the exports of Peru."

That was so not happening.

"Take out a pen or pencil," I said, "and write at least one paragraph about the many uses of the afro comb."

There was a stunned silence, so I slipped behind my desk and took out a pen and piece of paper of my own. "You've got thirty minutes," I said, and I started to write. Amazingly, my class did too. (Boy was I relieved!)

There are, it turns out, many, many uses for an afro comb, including picking your nose (but not your friend's nose) and defending your girlfriend's honor; but for me, it got me writing again. I did everything my students did because it was the best way to get them going, and it re-inspired me. At age twenty-two, twelve years after my first attempt at writing fiction, I remembered that I had stories to tell. It was still a long road—my first story wasn't published until about five or six years later—and I wasn't able to start writing without having any other job until I was in my forties.

How did you get started?

Once I remembered how much I loved to write, I started writing short stories, sending them to magazines and receiving rejection letters—like, lots—and then one day I sent the right story to the right magazine, and they sent me a check. Hey, go figure—it was a story about a teenaged girl for a teen magazine. Hello! I'd only been teaching high school for the last seven years!

I kept doing that until there were a few magazines who knew who I was, and sometimes they would call and ask me to write a story or an article on a certain topic, and I would, and they would pay me. You wouldn't believe some of the topics. *Sweat* is one of my favorites, but they ranged from that to "What to do if you feel second-best to your sister." This went on for a while, and then I decided I wanted to write a book.

I partnered with another writer I knew, and we wrote a nonfiction book for kids about getting ready to be themselves and lead their own lives. We got it published. Then I felt like, *Whoa, I'm really a writer!* I wrote another book for teens, this time fiction. And it was published. I kept writing articles, stories, and books; and I did that while I was teaching English, getting a degree in theater, teaching theater and English, running a children's theater company, teaching just theater, and raising a daughter.

Whew!

Then one day, a publisher asked me if I wanted to write a series of books for kids—boys and girls, ages eight to twelve. "What do kids that age like to read about?" I asked Marijean, who at the time was thirteen or fourteen and thus closer to that particular stage than I was at forty-something.

"History," she said. I raised my eyebrows, thinking lists of dates and black-and-white pictures of dead guys with big mustaches.

"Different clothes, different stuff, wild animals, runaway carriages, wars, disease, riding horses, random people with guns, undiscovered countries..." She gave me that teenage girl look.

"Got it," I said. So I proposed a series of books that followed one family through almost three centuries of American history, from Salem, Massachusetts, to Oxford, Mississippi.

The proposal became the Christian Heritage Series.

By the time I finished writing the Santa Fe Years, a man had come up with an idea for a series of books for eight- to twelve-year-old girls. He'd really just thought of a name for a girl he wanted someone to write about—Lily. He called a friend of his, who happened to be my agent, and asked, "Do you know anyone who could write a series of books like this?"

"Nancy Rue," said my agent. (Bless his heart!)

By the time the Lily Series was born, I was writing full-time. I was eventually able to stop writing stories and articles, and just focus on books.

So I guess the really, really short answer is that I got started writing by writing, and I got started as a paid writer by being persistent about trying to sell my writing and doing a good job for the people who came to depend on me. And what I've learned is that the more you do what you love to do, the more other people seem to want you to do it.

How cool is that?

Why did you decide to start writing Christian books?

When I first started writing for publication, I imagined my writing appearing in *Redbook*, *Woman's Day*, *Ladies Home Journal*, and every other popular women's magazine I'd seen in the grocery store check-out line. My stories came back almost as fast as I sent them out. Those big-time magazines usually go searching for famous authors to submit fiction, and they have writers on staff for their articles. I just kept writing though, and one day I finished a story about a teenager. I was looking for a place to send it, knowing it wasn't exactly *Redbook* material, and found a small Methodist magazine for teens. They sent me back an envelope, but it wasn't a rejection letter — it was a check.

Yeah, baby!

So when I did start to write books, that was the kind of book I chose ... or maybe it chose me. Before the Christian Heritage Series, I published four Christian books for and about teens. But it wasn't just because I knew I could publish them that those were the books I decided to write. When that first story actually made it to print, I took it as a message ... as God saying, "Hello! This is what you should be doing!" So, I did.

Are any of your books not a Christian book?

Early in my career, I wrote a novel for teens about dating violence — you read the girl's side of the story, then turned the book over and read the boy's side. It wasn't a Christian publishing company, so none of the characters were Christians, but I felt like it was still an important topic for teens. The principles, the things the characters learned, were things Jesus would be proud of. I also wrote several nonfiction books, things like "How to Pursue a Career in Hotels, Motels, and Resorts," and "Coping with an Illiterate Parent."

The way I look at it, there are three kinds of books:

1. Christian books that come right out with a message about Jesus Christ.
2. Books that give us information or stories about things that don't talk about Jesus directly, but encourage the

kinds of things that would please Jesus. They might even have messages of giving and love, which is what Jesus is all about, without coming right out and using his name.

3. And then there is decidedly un-Christian media, which glorifies the types of things we learn in the Bible are not good for us. I would never write, nor would I encourage anyone else to write, anything falling into this third category.

What was your favorite subject in school?

It was always English—anything that had to do with reading. I actually wasn't so crazy about the writing part of things until later, because especially in elementary school, teachers could be awfully picky about things like the size of the period you put at

The next day when they got to their combined English/history class, Ms. Hess, one of the two team teachers, was writing on the board in handwriting as bubbly as her voice:

Essay Assignment: YOUR Code of Honor

All other thoughts left Sophie's head. *I could write that essay in my sleep!* she thought.

"What's a Code of Honor?" Colton Messik said.

You wouldn't know one if it bit your head off, Sophie thought. For Pete's sake—they had only been studying the legends and the history of medieval times for three weeks. She had wondered more than once how Colton had ever gotten into this special honors block in the first place.

(from *Sophie Breaks the Code*)

the end of a sentence. Once, in the third grade, I decided I was going to make mine really big and black. I was actually humiliated in front of an entire class by the principal, who was visiting our classroom and held my paper up, saying, "Look at these periods at the end of her sentences! Now, isn't that ridiculous?" No wonder I was afraid to write. But I have always, always, always loved to read.

On your website you said that middle school years were hard for you. Why was that?

A lot of reasons, actually.

First of all, these were the years when I felt the absolute worst about my appearance. I was about a foot taller than everyone else in my class, my feet felt like someone had permanently welded snowshoes to the end of my legs, and my nose was so large I was

---

"Leo, don't let it touch you, man! It'll burn your skin off!"

Shad Shifferdecker grabbed his friend's arm and yanked him away from the water fountain just as Lily Robbins leaned over to take a drink. Leo barely missed being brushed by Lily's flaming red hair.

Lily straightened up and drove her vivid blue eyes into Shad.

"I need for you to quit making fun of my hair," she said through her gritted teeth. She always gritted her teeth when she talked to Shad Shifferdecker.

(from *Here's Lily!*)

---

afraid if I turned around too quickly I would take someone out with it. My mother made all my clothes, and while she was a very talented seamstress, they tended to reflect her desire that I remain forever four years old. She also cut my hair, keeping it very short and unable to be styled in any way, which made my enormous nose seem even more like a weapon of mass destruction.

Second, these were the years when most people's social lives started to pick up some speed — I know it happens a lot earlier now! People began to have parties. Girls started to be interested in boys, and vice versa. Due partially to my less-than-magazine-cover-like appearance and tendency to lodge the infamous nose comfortably within the pages of whatever book was nearest at hand, I was rarely invited to the kinds of gatherings where you needed some all-important social skills: batting eyelashes (I looked like I had something in my eyes); blushing attractively when teased (I closely resembled a tomato); giggling in a feminine and enticing way (I shrieked, with the occasional snort); tossing hair coquettishly (mine was cut like I was about to ship out with the troops); moving gracefully across crowded rooms (hello, klutz!); fixing my face in a mask of total fascination while *he* drones on and on about something very masculine and of absolutely zero actual interest (I fell asleep); dancing that crazy new dance that came out five minutes ago (see klutz); magically knowing all the current slang, trends, bands, movies, and everything that had ever crossed the television screen (huh? TV what the who, now?). Quite frankly, I was still perfectly content to read Nancy Drew over and over again, wear pajamas with feet, and confide in my favorite dolls when I was twelve — information that, if leaked, would have made me the fanny of every joke at Jefferson Davis Junior High School.

Third, while I was going through all of these issues that seemed pretty huge to me, my family was going through a very painful time. My father, who was a diabetic, was not doing well at all. Diabetes wasn't so easy to take care of then. The medications that allow many diabetics to live normal lives today did not exist, and though my daddy was very careful about his health, he started to lose his eyesight, and then he went completely blind. I adored my father—he was practically my best friend. It was devastating to see him go through that.

And finally, as difficult as it is to go through middle school in any era, the early 1960s were a very frightening time to be alive. All around us, in our pretty little houses full of tradition and Tupperware, people were struggling with very serious questions. Americans were still very afraid of communism, a political theory that opposes democracy. Both President John F. Kennedy and Dr. Martin Luther King, Jr. were assassinated. Desegregation was happening in my very neighborhood, and there was a lot of racial tension. Women were starting to work outside the home, even if they had children, which was a whole new thing. A lot of the world I knew from birth to twelve was changing and falling away, and it was scary to me.

It was definitely a time that shaped a lot of who I am. I think current events are a big influence on all twelve-year-olds. But for me especially, struggling with hard things at home gave me compassion for other people going through hard times, and I think it's why I enjoy writing for tweens as much as I do.

What are some of your favorite books?

I've already talked about a lot of books I loved as a kid—all those mysteries—but I will always have a very special place in my heart for *Anne of Green Gables* by L. M. Montgomery. I loved the character of Anne with her imagination and all her misadventures, and I loved reading about another time and place.

In college and graduate school, I really, really loved books by

F. Scott Fitzgerald and Ernest Hemingway. American writing from the 1920s is rich in description but at the same time simple. I was impressed by that.

When Marijean was in college, she got me started on Jane Austen. I think a lot of things the young women in her books go through still happen—falling in love, making social boo-boos, being embarrassed by your family, being driven nuts by brothers and sisters, etc.—and I also love how she can make a sentence go on for miles. No really—MILES.

Right now, though, I have more modern favorites—novels and nonfiction. *The Message*, Eugene Peterson's modern interpretation of the Bible, definitely tops the list. It has absolutely, without a doubt, changed my life, deepened my faith, and driven my ministry. I actually don't think I had a clear and full understanding of who Jesus was until I read *The Message*. Jesus, I found out, really gets us in a way we can't even get ourselves. Eugene Peterson's book helped me fall in love with our Lord Christ.

On the lighter side, I do still enjoy a good novel, and, of course, a good mystery—Nancy Drew dies hard, you know? I've been known to devour John Grisham books in a matter of days. One of my new favorite authors is Jodi Picoult. She's a good storyteller, but what I like best is that her characters learn about who they are through overcoming really intense obstacles. Another female novelist I like is Susan Howatch. The people in her novels try to live their faith, but there's also always a mystery woven through, and the result is very rich and satisfying.

Now, these are not necessarily novels I am recommending to readers under the age of eighteen. If you think they sound good to you, you should run them by your parents and respect their opinions.

I have always loved biographies too. Eleanor Roosevelt is a person I have recently been reading tons about, and she also wrote a few books, including one called *You Learn by Living*, which is one of my favorites. I also really enjoyed reading Gore Vidal's *Lincoln* and Arthur Miller's autobiography. Those are pretty thick—not books to fall asleep with, or you'll give yourself a concussion!

In a way, this is an impossible question to fully answer. At this point in my life, I usually have more than one going at a time—a fiction, a nonfiction, something about Christianity, books to research for what I'm writing about, and I also read parts of the Bible every day. Almost every single one has had an impact on me, because that's what books do—they get inside your head and change something about you.

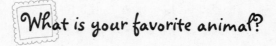 What is your favorite animal?

We didn't have animals when I was growing up, although I've always, you know, thought they were cute and fun. I did, however, marry into a family of animal lovers. My husband grew up with dogs, cats, a parakeet, and even a duck named Lucy.

We've had many pets over the years—dogs, cats, birds, fish, and for a short time my husband lived and worked on a ranch where endangered animals raised in captivity can retire; and I got to interact with everything from snakes to spider monkeys. I've fed a tiger a bottle, and I was bitten by a baby snow leopard.

Of course, if you've ever met me or been to my house, you would notice that there are frogs everywhere. I never travel without at least a small stuffed animal or figurine of a frog, and my office is completely frog-themed. People know that I collect them and they send them to me for every birthday and gift-giving holiday, and I buy every frog-themed greeting card I come across so I can send them to people. But when it comes to in-the-flesh, animal/person interaction, I confess I'm not that open to frogs.

They're adorable, don't get me wrong. They're also, you know, slippery, and they move really fast and unpredictably, and they eat bugs. I prefer something that licks your face to something that lands on it with little, sticky froggy feet. Sticky, jumpy, buggy things have been known to make me, you know, squeal really loud.

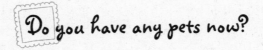

Do you have any pets now?

As you probably know by now, yes, I do, and I'll take any opportunity to talk about them for longer than you want to listen.

First there's Captain Sam, our yellow lab. He's only thirteen weeks old, but he already has a personality of his own. He will chase a tennis ball until he falls over, and if he ever grows into his feet, he's going to be a very big dog. I mean, very big. He already knocks things over just walking across the room.

His brother is Sullivan, named after a character in my books for grown-ups. We call him Sully, because Sullivan is a pretty long name for a dog so small. He's only eight weeks old, and right now he looks like a stuffed animal you'd get in your Christmas stocking. He is so black that you can't see his eyes from a distance or in pictures. Although he only weighs twelve pounds and Captain weighs twenty-two, he holds his own in puppy-wrestling competitions. He's a talker; we just don't know what he's saying. Yet.

What do you like most about being an author?

While my favorite part of being a *writer* is making up stories and characters and watching them take on a life of their own on the page, my favorite part of being an *author* is how readers actually get to connect with my writing. I love it when readers write to me and let me know what they liked (or sometimes what they didn't like) and how what they read affected them. I love it that, because I'm fortunate enough to be able to publish my ideas and viewpoints and creations, and other people learn and have fun and change, like I do when I read a book. The best, the best, the BEST is when a girl writes to me and tells me that one of my books really helped her through a hard time or helped her figure out how she could get to know God better. For me, that is what being an author is all about.

Do you have any brothers and sisters?

Here's the scoop on my brother, Billy, and my sister, Phyllis.

Billy was about ten when I was born. (I was kind of a surprise — actually I still like to surprise people.) He used all of his big-brother-torture-type stuff on Phyllis, who was seven when I was born, so all I remember about him was that he was nice to me, and played games with me, and was handsome and funny, like my dad.

I have to remember him from a child's viewpoint because he died when he was seventeen, and I was seven. He went to a party with some friends, and afterward they were drag racing. All I know about the accident is that he was thrown out of the car — I think it stopped suddenly and he wasn't wearing a seat-belt. Of course, this was very, very sad for my family; but I was pretty young, and no one would explain to me what was going on because they didn't think I would understand, so most of what I know about him or what happened comes from stories my mother and sister told me. So I know he was athletic — he liked to water ski and do chin-ups on the door frames — and smart, and a big kidder.

My sister, Phyllis, was the cool, fashionable, rebellious member of our family — and when I say rebellious, I mean she did things like shave her legs and wear lipstick when my mother told her not to. She lived at home until she got married, and didn't go to college, so when I was a teenager I had this cool, older sister in her twenties who drove a 1963 Volkswagen Beetle and showed me how to, well, shave my legs and wear lipstick; and she took my side when my mother still wanted to dress me like Strawberry Shortcake.

I don't remember us really fighting, because, remember, she was seven years older than I was. When she was a little girl, I was like a doll for her to play with, and when she was a teenager, I didn't present much competition. I could talk to her about teachers, boys, and gossipy girls. (She and I *never* gossiped, of course!) We were really good friends.

Growing up, she was always the pretty one and I was always the smart one. As adults, we've both complained about how these labels kind of got unfairly applied to us and did a lot to shape us as kids. For example, I was forced to take piano lessons for, oh, seven years, and I never really liked them. Phyllis really wanted to learn to play the piano, but no one ever asked her if she'd like lessons — they just assumed she wouldn't be interested. The moral of that story is pretty girls might want to play the piano!

My sister still lives in Florida. She married a military man named Bruce McLawhorn, who ended up sort of adopting a Navy buddy from California named Jim Rue (you can see where that's going). My sister and Bruce had two children — Billy (named for our brother and our father, whose name was also William) and Kristen. Billy and Kristen both have children now, so family gatherings can be, to say the least, eventful at the McLawhorn residence.

Phyllis and I are very close — we talk at least once a week, we see each other as often as we can, and she can always make me laugh. She also reads all of my books, and she always says they're wonderful. Everyone needs a sister like that.

What is your favorite food?

My all-time favorite food is chocolate—hands down, no question! I love chocolate so much ... I eat it every day. I buy this really dark, 70% cocoa, organic chocolate—bars and powder—and I eat a piece every day at lunch. I make a cup of hot chocolate with the powder at some point every day too. I actually just ate a piece right now because I was writing about it, and it made me really want some. Mmmmmm, chocolate.

Chocolate is actually good for you, especially if you're female. It's full of antioxidants, which can help prevent cancer, and it stimulates the serotonin in your brain, which is the chemical that regulates your happy/sad feelings. Every woman should (for health reasons, of course) eat a piece of dark chocolate every day. Really. Tell your mom I said so.

Do you have lots of hobbies?

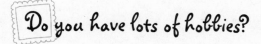

It seems like all I do is read, write, sleep, and eat. Okay, not ALL—I walk the puppies, I hang out with my family, and watch crime-solving shows on TV, and I travel ... to talk about reading and writing, so that doesn't really count as a separate category. My husband and I have a boat which we are out on even when it's forty degrees outside.

There are also things I enjoy doing, like decorating my house, for instance. I like it when I see pictures in magazines and then I find just that same pillow or lamp or something that same color, and I put it in a room in my house, and it looks great. I also have grand ideas of scrapbooking. I have lots of pictures of family and friends, that need to be taken out of trunks and old albums where the plastic sheet adheres to the sticky backing, and lots of

Lily felt herself deflating, kind of like a bicycle tire with a slow leak.

"Aren't you happy for me, Mom?" she said.

"Of course I am," Mom said. There was a "but" coming, though. Lily could tell by the way Mom tightened her ponytail and then folded her hands on the tabletop.

"I just want you to think about this," Mom said. "You already have Girlz Only club, plus you're going to want to be in the Shakespeare Club production again in the spring."

"But—"

"Plus you need time for studying and church activities." Mom gave Lily another long look. "I just don't want you spreading yourself too thin. You know how you go after things two hundred percent."

"But I can do it all, Mom!" Lily said.

(from *Lily Rules*)

memorabilia, including letters from readers that I would like to immortalize in super-cute ways on that beautiful paper with all those little do-dads from the Sassy Scrapper. Most of the time I look at the albums and the trunks and think, "Well, maybe when I retire ..."

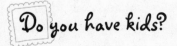

Do you have kids?

Yes! And I'm so glad you asked. I have one (incredible) kid, Marijean Suzanne Rue. She was born in 1979. As you probably have read at this point, she worked for me for a while—and we taught mother/daughter workshops together. She really helped me build my ministry for you.

Marijean is also my best friend. I actually don't know how that happened — I didn't bribe her or anything. We've just always connected in a way that sings. We've never been known to have nasty word fights, throw things, or stop speaking to each other for days on end. Marijean had her moments of "rebellion" when she refused to listen to Fleetwood Mac and didn't want to wear dresses to church. But for the most part, she's been a great part of the mother/daughter duo.

Marijean is tall and thin and has long brown hair that is straighter than straight — the hair I wanted in college, basically. She's married now and lives about an hour away from me. She and her husband, Brian, sometimes bring all three of their dogs to visit us. Can you even imagine the barking and slobbering?

She also loves to read, and she remembers stuff like you can't believe. She was a very good actress in high school, especially when it came to Shakespeare. And in college she discovered dance and loves all forms, from modern to African to belly dance. She sews — like my mother and sister — and also inherited that knitting-needlepoint-crafty thing that escapes me. She cooks like her grandmother from the other side of the family — no recipes, never the same twice, always good — and she's very health-conscious.

I could tell you LOTS more, of course, like how angry she gets when something is unfair. When she was six, we saw a program on TV in which ranchers were poisoning groundhogs, which dig holes that cattle step in and hurt themselves. Marijean was VERY upset about this. Later that day, the entire house was plastered with newly-markered posters: "SAV THE GROONDHOGS!!!!" "JUSTIS 4 GROONDHOGS!!!!!!!!!" Moments like that are pretty funny when I look back, but they also make me so proud of her generosity and strong sense of what is right.

What's your day like?

Let me see ...

My husband and I get up in the morning between 4:00 and 5:30 a.m., because the puppies are ready to get on with the day. I feed everyone of the four-legged variety and start the coffee. My husband leaves for work sometime before 6:00 a.m. — not because he has to, mind you, just because he likes to get there early — and I do my quiet time, which includes writing in a journal, reading from the Bible, praying, and stretching. I also eat some oatmeal.

I take the puppies for a walk. Sullivan can't go far yet because his legs are so short, so I have to carry him some of the way. I then hop into the shower where I discover that the plastic frogs that stick to the wall with suction cups have been completely re-arranged in bizarre configurations by Jim at 5:00 a.m.

Then I check my email and direct dog traffic until they drop wherever they stand and fall into puppy sleep. That's when I start my writing day. I work and take puppies out and bring them in and work and play with puppies and work. Are you getting that writing is a lot of work? (And that puppies are too?) It's sometimes hard to stop for lunch because I get so involved with my characters, but I do make a big ol' salad with lots of stuff in it. My mind keeps going on the next scene I'm going to write, so when I get back to my desk, I can start right in again. Except that I always say first, "I need a piece of chocolate," and I get the bar I keep in my desk drawer, break off a piece, and savor it. Chocolate has to be held in your mouth for a minute, you know.

At almost 5:00, I make snacks for Jim. When Jim gets home, we sit on the couch and tell each other about the day — the funny things, the stuff that drove us nuts, the things we've been saving up to share because it isn't totally lived until you've shared it with a friend. We call that happy hour.

Jim and I make dinner—I usually do most of the chopping, but he likes to stir-fry and grill things. We try to eat at the table, but sometimes the couch sucks us in. Whether we eat there or not, we always end up there after dinner. Jim flips through hundreds of satellite channels, and I dig through my pile of magazines and books and find something to read. I usually fall asleep, and Jim wakes me up around 9:00, and we go down to bed. Oh, and Marijean usually calls at least once to tell us something funny her animals did, her husband said, or she saw on TV.

Those are the writing days. There are also days when I go to my breakfast club, or interview people for my books, or spend time reading in the library or writing in a coffee shop. Doesn't it sound like a nice life? I'm so grateful to God for it.

Where did you and your husband meet?

I was not the first person in my family to meet Jim Rue, my husband. Introducing me to Jim was one of the many wonderful things my sister, Phyllis, has done for me.

Phyllis married Bruce McLawhorn, who was in the Navy. Bruce met a twenty-year-old kid from California named Jim. Jim was tall, skinny, and blonde, and lonely being so far away from family and friends. Bruce used to take Jim home for real food, which is, of course, how Jim met Phyllis. Often Jim would end up sleeping on their couch, and sometimes watching their kids. One night, Phyllis showed Jim a picture of her little sister.

"I don't ever want to meet her," Jim said and handed the picture back to Phyllis.

"Why not?" Phyllis said—more than just a little bit huffy. Hello!

"Because," Jim said, "she's the kind of girl you marry—and I'm never getting married!"

Tee-hee.

When I did meet Jim, at his 21st birthday party, I saw right away that he was like the Energizer Bunny. Everything he did had a purpose, even if it was just to embrace his inner silliness. And, in fact, as the evening went on and we talked over dinner, I found out he brought out MY inner silliness! I thought I was being absolutely hilarious, and his laughter got all mixed up with mine until it was hard to tell whose was whose. Interesting, huh, how I had more fun with him than I usually had with the boyfriend I had at the time?

Fortunately for me, Jim was already pretty much a fixture at Phyllis and Bruce's house, so when my mother and I went to their house, Jim would always be there. Nobody could make me laugh like Jim did. He could walk across a room and do a fake fall and I was doubled over. That grew into writing to each other when he was overseas with the Navy. It was my patriotic duty, right? In the summer between my senior and junior years of college, when I broke up with my boyfriend, Jim heard it from Phyllis and apparently started making plans. The short version is that on our first date we danced the beer barrel polka and fell in love. Yes, that's our song—"Roll Out the Barrel." You might NOT want to tell your mom that!

"Is this a Catholic church?" Lily asked.

"No, this is the Church of England," Mrs. Benedict said. "It's an Anglican Church, like your Episcopal Church in the U.S."

"Isn't that like Catholic?" Lily said.

"Only in that we both use beautiful ceremony in our worship. But this church is very Protestant indeed." Her eyes twinkled at Lily. "Don't let on to anyone that I told you."

(from *Lily's in London?!*)

A few weeks later the man I had fallen in love with—fallen like a big ol' tree—asked me to marry him, and all I could do was bob my head up and down. And you know what? He still leaves me speechless sometimes.

What church do you go to?

I'm an Episcopalian, born and raised, which means I'm a member of the Anglican Communion or the Church of England. That's the church the Pilgrims were trying to break away from when they came to America, but we've come a long way since then.

I really like the Episcopal Church because we follow an outline during each service, which is called a *liturgy*. This is very meaningful to me, as well as familiar (which shouldn't be surprising, since I've been hearing it almost every Sunday for over fifty years!). Our priests and other people helping out with the service wear special robes, and there's an altar up at the front of the church where the priest prepares the Eucharist, or Communion, every Sunday.

Because I have a pretty big ministry of my own outside of church, I need a church where I can have my well filled. Does that make sense? Sometimes as Christians we need to step out of the meetings and the activities and the obligations and make sure we are really worshiping and growing and learning as Christians on the inside. So I now attend St. Augustine's Chapel on the Vanderbilt Campus in Nashville. St. Augustine's is both Methodist and Episcopalian, so sometimes the Episcopal priest runs the service and sometimes the Methodist minister does. I learn a lot, I get to serve at the altar sometimes, I love the people I worship with, and I always leave feeling like I've just been in the house of God. In addition to the prayers and hymns I grew up with, there is often someone with a guitar singing a Beatles' song, and the Episcopal priest always does the service in bare feet. But I think the experience is just what it's supposed to be. And the best part? St. Augustine's has a mission — several in fact. We have a hospice in Africa, a sister church and a school in Ecuador, and five houses (count them, five!) for women who have been drug addicts and who are now productive members of the community. God is at work at St. Augustine's, and that inspires me to do the work he has given me to do with gladness and singleness of heart.

When is your birthday?

My birthday is July 27. I love birthdays, and I never mind turning a year older. I usually spend the whole day looking back at the last year, celebrating all my secret delights and thinking about how I want to grow in the next year. It's just so good — this being a person thing.

If you weren't an author, what would you be?

Well, we know that if I had not taken the leap to be a full-time author, I'd probably still be teaching public high school (shudder!) or, perhaps, I'd have gone into running a theater company with my husband full-time. We did that for a few years while we were attending the University of Nevada in Reno and getting our theater degrees.

But if we're just dreaming here, and I could choose anything in the world, I'd be a backup singer for someone like Tina Turner, Aretha Franklin, or Diana Ross. Actually, funny thing, right before we got to this question, Marijean and I were in a coffee shop working, and they were playing "Stop! In the Name of Love!" by the Supremes. We burst into the lyrics (we knew ALL the words, of course) and did hand motions (pretending we were wearing long gloves) right there at the table while the funky-haired, multi-pierced employees looked on. We've actually spent quite a bit of time over the years perfecting our routines on car trips and in the kitchen—various hand motions, kick ball change, and grapevine steps. We harmonize really well. The oldies station was the only radio station our family could all agree on when we were together, so there isn't a song out there written between 1955 and 1975 that we don't have some kind of shoo-bop number for.

Do you have any family members who write too?

My father wrote poetry. I have some of his poems, which are very special to me, especially one he wrote for my mother. Who knew a dad could be so romantic? He and I shared a love of reading, and I think if he'd lived longer I could have gotten him to spend more time on his poetry and maybe even branch out a little.

I love seeing Marijean blossoming as a writer, and it's exciting to think that my grandchildren, whenever they decide to arrive, will have lots of opportunities to develop whatever their talents are. Who knows—they might turn out to love writing too. But we're also a family full of athletes, artists, and—on Marijean's husband's side—intellectuals and business owners. Those are going to be some SPECIAL grandkids.

(I wish they'd hurry it up though!)

What's your favorite Scripture?

But whoever did want him, who believed he was who he claimed and would do what he said, He made to be their true selves, their child-of-God selves.

—JOHN 1:12–13 *THE MESSAGE*

I base my whole ministry and all the books I write on this one Scripture. It is totally central to my faith. I think that believing in God, as revealed by Jesus and the writings in the Old Testament, leads us to live a Christian life, which means peeling away all the false-self things that we develop because of the unsafe world we live in. When all those false-self things — like being mean or gossipy or insecure or angry all the time — are gone, we're left with the God-self, the self God made us to be on this earth, each with our own special purpose. I think a Christian life is the PROCESS of becoming this true, God-made self. We're never going to be perfect. This is a journey we're on — following God's instructions that Jesus lays out so well for us and discovering the God-self more and more each day.

It's a journey I've been on for a while now, and I know I will be on it until I die. It's a lot of work, but, yikes, is it worth it!

When did you first become a Christian?

I was baptized into the Episcopal Church as an infant and raised in it all my life. Back then, you couldn't take Communion until you were confirmed, and you couldn't be confirmed until you were twelve. I had to take special classes to learn about all the symbolism and traditions of the Anglican denomination so I would understand what Episcopalians believe and practice. At my confirmation I wore a white dress and shoes and a veil, and the bishop of the diocese (a diocese is a region that a bishop is responsible for) said a special blessing over me. It was a huge rite of passage in my congregation and my family, and it was very meaningful. You could definitely say that was the day I officially became an Episcopalian.

But I was definitely a Christian before that. Christianity was a huge part of my life long before I was twelve, and I always remember believing in and loving God. My family really kept me focused on the Christian life even when I was distracted with school and friends through high school and college. My mother and sister were steeped in the traditions of the church, and my father was a deeply spiritual person. I never questioned whether or not I should be on a Christian path or whether or not I should have a relationship with God. That relationship has always been through the Bible and the Church, even before I was confirmed.

So while I can remember moments, like my confirmation, when I grew in my faith as a Christian, I can't really pinpoint when I became a Christian. I don't remember asking Jesus into my heart, but I always remember Jesus being there with me. Now, as a grown-up, I am much more aware of the importance of following Jesus' teachings than I was at some younger times in my life. I think that means there is more and more of Jesus in me every day. The Christian life is a process of becoming who God made me to be, and "when I became a Christian" was probably the moment I started on that path. I was just born into a time and family and Christian tradition where that path started before I can really remember, and I've gradually grown more aware of it as I've grown more aware of myself. When you think about it, that's a testimony in itself, isn't it?

What makes you nuts?

Oh my ... Wow, so many things! Actually, I think I've really mellowed over time, because I can think of a lot of things that used to drive me crazy and I've been able to let them go. I'm too busy on my journey to spend the energy it takes to get annoyed about a bunch of trivial stuff. However, I still have some favorites.

Number one on my list, without question, is when people are rude. You know, calling people names or shoving their way to the front because it's oh, so important to be first. Closely related to that is when people are inconsiderate. You know, so concerned with what they need and want that they don't consider what other people might need and want, which usually leads them to being rude. We can all be inconsiderate when we don't mean to be; it's the people who don't seem to care when they are rude that make me want to rip out someone's nose hairs with red hot tweezers.

On the more trivial side, I can't stand my daughter biting her nails, my husband flipping the channels (don't you hate that?), music that repeats over and over and over (like "The Twelve Days of Christmas"), and my dog looking right at me and then walking the other way when I'm standing there screaming, "Captain! Come here!"

But you know what drives me nuttier than anything? When people turn Christianity into a list of rules, of do's and don'ts, instead of focusing on God's love and grace—something Jesus talks about in every Gospel over and over and over. That makes me crazy-mad because it turns people off from the good news

"Where's my sock?" Brooke said, pawing through the pile she'd just dumped. "I can't find my sock."

"Maybe you dropped it on the way from your locker." Willoughby glanced at Sophie and added, "Want me to help you look?"

"I'll just borrow one." Brooke straightened up to face them. "Anybody got an extra sock?"

Sophie pulled out her special toe socks, the ones with the turtles on the bottom. "You can borrow these. I don't need socks with my boots—"

"Sweet!" Brooke said, and swept them out of Sophie's hand. She was feeding her toes into them before Sophie could finish her sentence.

(from *Sophie's Encore*)

Jesus has to offer, and it gives a bad name to those of us really trying to live the love and the grace part, because we also call ourselves Christians.

Which three people have had a positive impact on your life?

There are certainly a lot more than three people who have brought out the best in me, but I can certainly choose three who stand out pretty significantly.

First and foremost, there's my father, William Theodore Naylor, Jr. Until he died when I was fourteen, he was the center of my universe. I looked like him — long pointy nose, brown eyes, big ol' mouth. We had a lot of the same personality traits, like being easily moved to tears and having very strong likes and dislikes. I could talk to him about anything — and usually did, probably longer than he could listen to me.

My dad called me "Butch-o-Mio," and always tried to make me laugh. I've mentioned that he was very spiritual and committed to the church, and I learned a lot about being a Christian from him. He was thoughtful and sensitive. He never failed to ask me how my day was, and then actually listened to my answer. Because he got so sick, he could be very vulnerable, but he was graceful about it, noble, because he wasn't afraid to ask for help. He worked very hard to make a good life for my family, but he wasn't always working. We played board games, went water skiing, took a family vacation to New Jersey every year, and ate a lot of spaghetti.

My dad inspired me to strive to be my best self. He made me feel that who I was — smart, a bookworm, skinny, goofy — was always a great way to be, and he taught me about being gentle and loving. He always made me feel safe, because he was so sure of what was right and what was wrong. But he wasn't strict; he wasn't about rules. He taught me how to make good choices based on what I just knew was right, and I modeled what was right after him. Even though he has been gone for more than forty years, I still miss him.

Next would have to be my friend, Zondra. I've known *about* Zondra since my first year of college, because she was the freshman Beauty Queen. I spent a fair amount of time admiring Zondra from a distance, listening to guys around me talk about how stunning she was, and generally feeling like I could never measure up to someone like her.

I actually *met* Zondra right before the start of my senior year, when I, the head resident of my dorm, was in my apartment preparing for freshman orientation week and she, the assistant head resident in my dorm, came bursting in. She told me her ceiling was leaking, and she could not live in a leaky room, and she was adamant on that point! I could really like a girl who would actually use the word *adamant* in a sentence. We became friends very quickly, because we spent approximately 24 hours a day together—trying to take care of 300 freshmen girls who seemed determined to try marijuana, come in late, and at one point burn the building down (I'm serious).

After college, even though we ended up in different parts of the country for the next sixteen years, we stayed in touch, supporting each other through early marriage, motherhood, teaching careers, and the general craziness of life.

Zondra wasn't a perfect person, and she hadn't had a perfect life. She could be as insecure and feel as unattractive as I could, in spite of her beauty. And when I figured that out, Zondra became even more of an ally. Zondra was one of the first friends that I could share my weaknesses with as well as my strengths. Through her friendship, I've learned a lot about myself and about God.

We usually talk more than once a day. Probably the best thing about Zondra is she's like an adult and a little kid at the same time, and no matter what either one of us is going through, we can still make each other laugh like college girls. Zondra has taught me that beauty truly resides in the spirit and shines when we are living God's love.

I considered a lot of people for my third person—certainly my husband, Jim, and my daughter, Marijean, could have easily been two of my choices—but I decided to talk about my Aunt La. Aunt La, or Laura Danley, knew me from the time I was born until I was 48, when she died in her seventies. Aunt La was not actually my blood relative, but she expanded my idea of family. I was closer to her than to any of my actual aunts. This was probably because Aunt La was a naturally loving person and she never had any kids of her own. She loved with her whole heart whatever children came into her world, including me. To her, everyone was a brother, sister, or child of hers in God's family.

Aunt La, or La-La, as we sometimes called her, survived her sometimes difficult life by focusing on the small, positive things that she could control. Her husband didn't like to travel, but she would take small jobs, save her own money, and take trips to visit us. She didn't have much money for clothes or decorating, so she filled her house with beautiful things she stitched. She was lonely sometimes, so she sang in the choir, volunteered at schools and libraries, and wrote letters every day. And instead of dwelling on things she didn't like about her life, she kept a gratitude journal. When she died and I went through her things, I found it. Every day, the first thing she wrote was, "I am grateful for Nancy." Every single day, even on the days I didn't write to her or didn't call or couldn't be there.

When I read that, I truly realized what family means. It's the people God gives you to love, and whom you love unconditionally. Sometimes you're related to them, and sometimes you're not, but no matter what they do wrong or how far away they are, you find a way to be grateful for them and understand what's good about them. Aunt La had a great gift for that, and even more than all the fun and understanding and love she gave me, that's the gift I'm most grateful for.

Is it amusing when people think you're Nancy Drew?

You know, now that you ask this question, I can't think of a time this has ever really happened to me. I think people often think they have heard of me because the name Nancy Rue sounds vaguely like the name Nancy Drew, which is infinitely more famous.

I really don't think, not in a million years, that anyone would ever really mistake me for the savvy, graceful, accomplished, witty, blonde, stylish, roadster-driving, crime-solving Nancy Drew. And that is 100% okay with me — because she is not real. She is as unreal as any romance-novel heroine, TV sitcom character, or magazine-cover model that anyone ever thought she needed to be, to be cool, popular, liked, or loved. Me? I'm definitely real.

chapter two

The Girls

Answers to Pressing Sophie and Lily Questions

How many Lily books have you written? Are you writing one right now?

I haven't written a Lily book since, oh, 2002? There are fourteen Lily books in all, not counting the companion nonfiction books that went with them—add those in, and that makes twenty-six. And I LOVED writing them. Lily and I did a lot of growing together. She got older and more grown-up and learned a lot about being a young woman and a Christian, and I learned a lot about writing, a lot about girls today, and a lot about what I really want to do with my life.

I want to get the message out to every girl that she is uniquely and wonderfully created by God and she should strive to be her best self and never hide who she is. That wasn't easy for Lily. In fact, it isn't easy for anybody. God never promised that it would be easy to be authentic. What God does promise is that he's always there, nudging and guiding and comforting. Lily learned that—and so did I. (Which just goes to show, you are NEVER too ancient to learn!)

Do you like fashion models and all that stuff like you wrote about in *Here's Lily*?

Here's the thing: I think it's perfectly fine to look your best and be into fashion. I personally love great clothes, especially jeans with flowers embroidered down the leg and long flowing skirts and big belts that sort of hang lopsided over my hips. I think every female has her own beauty and that we honor God when we show that

"I think you've found your true self, Lil," Art said. "You know that 'you' that you've been looking for ever since you thought you were gonna be some fashion model?"

Lily nodded.

"The real Lily Robbins is this *très magnifique* person who is probably gonna do about a hundred different things with her life before she's through. But her true thing? It's always gonna be gathering up the details and sorting them out and doing what God tells her in that whole big basket of stuff only she and God understand." He shook his curly head. "Does that make any sense at all?"

"Yeah," Lily said, in a voice full of happiness-tears.

And it did. Of course it did.

Because it was a God thing.

(from *Lily's Passport to Paris*)

beauty in its best light. I even think fashion models are very cool, the way they make the camera work for them and those great clothes we love to buy. But there are two things I want to say about all of that.

One — even though it's fun and even important to look your best, appearance should never totally consume your life, you know what I mean? If you can't walk past a store window without stopping to examine your do or your pimple situation, that could mean you're a little too wrapped up in how you look. And if you pitch a fit when you have a bad hair day and practically refuse to go to school, yeah, that's a problem. My advice? LOOK your best — and then go BE your best.

Two — I REALLY have a problem with the way models function in our society today. Wherever you look — magazines, TV, movies, whatever — the people who design and produce the clothes and shows and advertising we see have sort of decided that only one kind of woman is beautiful, and that everyone should look like her. I don't think there was some kind of meeting that happened and everyone decided this. It happened over time. But I bet you can tell me what this ultimate woman looks like.

She's white, she's way tall, and she's scary-skinny. She has long, flowing hair, big breasts (in spite of the fact that the rest of her looks anorexic!), and her belly-button is exposed. She's wearing lots of makeup (we're talking put on with a putty knife), enough jewelry to start her own store, impressive shoes (which could also be used as weapons), and hardly any clothing. At least one very attractive member of the opposite sex is either hanging on her physically or drooling in her general direction, but she doesn't seem happy about it — in fact, she looks like she smells something bad, plus her eyes are half closed and her mouth is hanging open a little bit.

Yep, you've got it. That description can fit everyone from Tyra Banks to Jennifer Aniston — yes, even the "white" part. Very rarely do you see black women in magazines who don't have hair that has been processed to be soft and straight or skin that isn't on the lighter side of the spectrum. Most of the black women and girls I've worked with tell me they don't feel pressure so much to be thin as to "look more white." The thing is, African American, white, Asian, or Hispanic—it's really, really hard to look at those pictures in magazines or on TV and not wonder, "Hey, why don't I look like that?"

NOBODY looks like that! The girl under all that stuff is primped over for hours and hours by a whole team of people before she gets in front of a camera to make that what-is-that-smell? face. Once the photo is taken, another team goes to work on it with

> The best part came when they bought a pizza and smuggled it into Dad's room at Baptist Hospital. Dad had a pretty much nonstop smile himself as Mom popped pepperoni into his mouth and told him all about the show.
>
> "I have never been so proud of her," Mom said. "She was poised and graceful and all that—but it was the beauty that came from someplace inside her that really got to me."
>
> "It came from God," Lily said.
>
> There was a momentary disturbance as Art clapped his hand over Joe's mouth, but Dad didn't seem to notice. His face grew soft as he looked at Lily.
>
> "That certainly makes our decision easy, doesn't it?" he said to Mom.
>
> "Do you mean I can sign on with the modeling agency?" Lily said.
>
> "Absolutely. Your mom and I have seen a lot of God in what you're doing there. You can keep it up if you want to."
>
> (from Here's Lily!)

airbrushing and computer enhancing. They can slim her waistline, clear up her skin, and even give her a cute little mole above her lip if they want to. See that picture of me on the back cover of this book? I asked the photographer to whiten my teeth before he printed it for me! So—again—just to be sure you get it: absolutely no one is as perfect as that girl on the cover of GL appears to be. So don't even go there.

Why does anybody go there? Fashion designers and department stores, makeup companies and television and movie studios all buy into this everyone-the-same, really-hard-to-achieve kind of beauty because, very simply, it makes them money. When people feel pressure to look a certain way, when the advertising they see again and again and again promises that someone will like them if they look that way, they will spend the money on the products that promise to change the way they look.

Now, I, of course, use shampoo, conditioner, a couple different kinds of lotions, a shower gel, a shaving razor, and hairspray (cut me some slack—I grew up in the sixties!). I also wear some makeup. (I'm actually a lip gloss freak—you'll seldom see me without it. I have all colors.) Again, there's nothing wrong with putting time and energy into looking your best. We're girls—it feels good to do that! Plus, when you're going to meet someone for the first time, or to some special occasion, the effort you put into looking nice tells the person or people you're going to see that they are important to you. And for most girls, it's just fun to play with your hair and put things on your face and wear fun clothes. We're still finding cosmetics, wigs, jewelry, and the latest fashions in the tombs of Ancient Egypt, so the fact that girls like to look nice is not news.

I'd probably be a happier camper about the whole women-in-advertising thing if more types of beauty were represented, because EVERYONE is beautiful. No, that's really true. Every man, woman, and child is beautiful, physically, in some way, and that gets either enhanced or diminished by who they are inside. But until they develop a runway that our insides can strut on down, well, I'll just have to keep steering clear of *Vogue* and fighting the good fight.

What's your favorite part in the Lily books?

Let me put it this way—all books follow a formula, which I'll get into more in the chapter about writing. The Lily books are no exception. Here's how it works:

- The characters and setting get established.
- What the characters want gets established.
- Then there's something that gets in the way of what they want.
- The characters try several different things to remove that very irritating something and get what they want.

It was the longest afternoon in the history of middle school, Lily was sure of that. Every minute was like an hour as she chewed on what she was supposed to do, and when she got home, she was no closer to an answer.

"If I go to Reni's at six," she told Otto, "I won't have to worry about being grounded tonight. But that means I don't go to Ashley's, and if I don't go to Ashley's, I'm not cool and then the newspaper staff will make my life miserable, and I won't get to be Answer Girl anymore!"

Otto jumped down from the bed as if he had the perfect solution and came back with a slimy, defurred tennis ball, which he dropped into her lap.

"That is SO not helping," she said.

(from *Ask Lily*)

✎ In the end, they're either successful or they're not, but you, the reader, know how it all worked out, which makes it the end of the book — but not the end of my answer to this question.

In every book, Lily wants something — to be a model, to have a horse, to fix everyone's problems, to have the best party, whatever. And there's always one or several things that get in the way — parents, teachers (especially Mrs. Gooch and Deputy Dog), kids at school, like the ABCs and the always obnoxious Shad Shifferdecker, money, the weather, strange little dogs ... But, always, the toughest obstacle for Lily to deal with is the part of *herself* that's getting in the way.

My favorite part of every Lily book, regardless of which one it is, is the part when Lily realizes what part of herself is causing her current problems. It's after she comes to terms with whatever that thing is that she's able to confront and conquer the problems that she isn't causing. Because once she's grown as a person, she has the strength to face the bully, the meanie, or the stupidhead. But the part I like best is when she's way down, thinking, *Oh, I messed up!* because it's only uphill from there, baby!

Did any Christians inspire you to write the Lily books?

Funny thing about that — another Christian actually *told* me to *write* the Lily books.

Steve Arterburn is a Christian psychologist who started a nationwide chain of Christian counseling centers. He also founded the Women of Faith conferences for Christian women. Your mom may have been to one. People wrote books for women that were sold at those conferences. Steve, who had a daughter of his own, got to thinking, "Hey, we shouldn't just wait until women grow up to write books they can read!" All he knew was that he wanted someone to write books for Young Women of Faith. He wanted them to be about an eleven-year-old girl named Lily.

That was really as far as he got. Then, he called my agent, who happened to be his agent as well at the time, and asked who should write that book, and my agent said, "Nancy Rue."

Ya gotta love agents!

Anyway, my agent called me and asked me if I was interested, and I said, "Oh, I don't know — I don't think that's my thing." Then I told my husband, and he said, "Have you lost your mind?!?!?! Call that man back right now!!!!"

I love that guy too — but you heard all about that in the first chapter.

So I called my agent back and said I'd write a proposal. A proposal is a description of the main character, central themes of a book, some plot suggestions, and a section explaining who would buy it and read it. I sat down that night in the living room to watch TV, and suddenly she just came to me — it's like she was right there with me on the couch, just talking her head off. I grabbed a pencil and a pad of paper and got to work.

There were some other Christians who inspired me to write about Lily too. I didn't know it at the time, but they were out there, thousands of them: Christian girls who really needed someone to write about stuff on their terms. As I moved forward with the Lily series and started doing conferences for eight- to twelve-year-old girls, they became my inspiration for Lily, and later, Sophie, and then ... Lucy!

Are you like Lily at all?

Oh yeah! When I do something — and I've always been this way — I do it 150%. When I get into a thing, I want all the equipment, all the accessories, and all the books ever written about it—we call it "going whole hog." I can also be kind of bossy, like Lily. When I'm the leader of a group, I tend to just jump right in with "This is what we're going to do!" and I have to be really careful about that.

Like Lily, I wanted to make good grades, please my parents, and have everyone like me. Sometimes that's a good thing, but like Lily, it sometimes, even now, holds me back a little bit. None of us is good at absolutely everything. And if we try to please everybody else, we're going to get confused inside. I hope, like Lily, I'm continuing to learn when it's important to do what others think is good for me, and when I should do what I know is good for myself. God is the one who helps me figure that out, through prayer and Scripture study and that still, quiet voice.

Did you ever have a fire at your house?

No, but when Marijean was a junior in high school, her best friend's room caught fire—we still don't know how—and it was completely destroyed. Chamaea (that's pronounced Ka-May-Ah) was on her way to meet Marijean at another friend's house, and they were going to go to a dance. Chamaea's sister, Mairin (that's Mare-in) was home alone at the time, making macaroni and cheese. She smelled smoke and thought she'd spilled something on the burner. Fortunately a neighbor up the street saw the flames coming out of the house and came running to see if anyone was inside.

The fire department came very quickly. So, fortunately for the family, the entire house was not destroyed, but unfortunately for Chamaea, her whole room was.

Mairin and Chamaea moved in with Marijean and me (Jim was away working at the time). They lived with us for a couple of months, following our routine and having their own places for toothbrushes and their hair stuff. Because we were so freaked out by the experience, all four of us slept in the master bedroom in various makeshift beds. Sometimes I would wake up in the middle of the night and hear Chamaea crying. We'd talk for a while about how scary it all was and how blessed we felt to have what we did have.

Oddly enough, the whole thing was a really great experience. We got to spend a lot of really fun, healing time with people we now consider to be family members, and we learned firsthand how unimportant possessions really are.

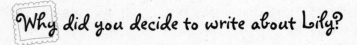

Why did you decide to write about Lily?

I decided to write about Lily because I had never, and have never since, had a character come to me so quickly and fully developed as she did. It was as though she was real, that I really had just discovered this eleven-year-old redhead in my house. And to me, that was a gift from God. It was one of those signs that this was what God wanted me to do.

So even though my husband provided me with a boost of confidence, I decided to write about Lily because God told me to. No, there was no actual voice I could hear. There was just a deep knowing. Besides, Lily just wouldn't leave me alone.

Why did you stop writing about Lily and start writing about Sophie?

Lily grew up! The Lily series actually went on much longer than the publisher and I originally planned, but readers were so responsive to the books that we ended up doing fourteen instead of the original six. But when you get to the fourteenth book, Lily is thirteen—an official teenager—and since these are supposed to be books for and about *tweens*, it was time for something new.

I was going to write the next series about Tessa, Lily's adopted sister, and Lily would kind of pop in and out as a featured character, but Zondervan decided they wanted the main character in the

---

"I guess Mama told you what happened," Sophie said.

"She did." Daddy pulled up the pink vanity stool and sat carefully on it. "What were you thinking, Soph?"

"I was thinking about a story I was making up," Sophie said. "And then all of a sudden, my group was gone. I guess I got carried away."

He blinked and ran his hand through his thick black hair. "At least you're honest."

I hope that counts when you start thinking up my punishment, Sophie thought.

"But you give me the same reason every time something like this happens."

"I couldn't help it," Sophie said. "You should see that place. Everything is exactly like it was back in the olden days—exactly!"

"Can you promise me that this won't happen again?"

Sophie thought about it, and then she shook her head.

"Why not?"

"Because—it just happens."

"And is it the same thing that 'just happens' when you stare into space in the classroom and don't get your work done?"

"Yes, sir."

Daddy's eyebrows pinched together. "Then we have to find a way to make it stop happening," he said.

(from *Sophie's World*)

---

next series to have a completely "blank page" and address really different issues.

Sophie was born out of the need to reach girls who are not outgoing hyper-overachievers like Lily, but who are actually quiet and maybe struggling to find out how to express themselves. It's not that girls like that couldn't read about Lily and still love the books, but there's a difference between reading about something that appeals to you and reading about somebody who's a whole lot like you. It's like the difference between reading about elephants in Africa and thinking that's really cool, and reading about golden retrievers, which you love because you have seven of them. For some girls, Lily is the elephant, and for some girls, Sophie is.

The other thing that's different about the Sophie series is that I really felt a need to focus on the issue of girl politics, or the unspoken rules about how girls interact. You'll notice that in every Sophie book, there are conflicts between friends (among the Corn Flakes), different friend groups (Corn Pops, Wheaties), and guys and girls (Fruit Loops, Lucky Charms). I did that not only because relationships with other people become a really big deal at your age, but also because the problems that come out of those relationships these days have become more and more serious, sometimes even a matter of life and death.

Now Sophie has grown up too, and there's one more series for eight- to twelve-year-old girls in me. The main character of that book—Lucy Rooney!—is going to be completely different from both Lily and Sophie. How do you think I'm going to manage that?

How can you love Sophie as much as Lily?

This question makes me think of a group called MOMYS (Mothers of Many Young Siblings). It's an online support group for mothers who homeschool their kids and have at least four children. Every year they hold a retreat in Williamsburg, Virginia, where the second series of the Christian Heritage books is set, and learn about Colonial America and the Revolutionary War. They take classes in everything from dancing to candle making to writing with a quill pen. I've been going for a couple of years now to give tours that help bring the Williamsburg books to life. I run around with all of these families, some of whom are comprised of ten children *or more*.

When I talk to the parents of these huge families, they know as much about the likes and dislikes, talents and shortcomings, fears and hopes, of each individual child as I did about Marijean when she was that age. They love each one as much as the next one, even the one that gets lost on the tour or throws a tantrum in the tea room.

My characters are like "other kids" for me. I have a special love for each of them as individuals. Getting to know them and telling their separate stories has been as exciting as watching my child grow up. And think about it this way: Don't you love BOTH of your parents? Do you have more than one friend?

Love, even when it's for an imaginary person, isn't a substance like water, yarn, or flour. It's not like you only have so much in the container of your heart, and once you pour out what's in there you have to go get more. It's hard for us to understand, because we get so preoccupied with the way things are in the material world, but love actually *increases* when you give it away. Even to characters in books.

Do you daydream like Sophie?

I do daydream a lot, and I always have … but not exactly like Sophie. I will find my mind wandering and making up things that would be fun or scary or interesting, but mostly about myself; and it doesn't usually take a force of nature to bring me back to reality.

Now, I will say that there have been occasions when I was so lost in thought that I lost touch with reality. When I went on research trips to write the Christian Heritage Series, someone always had to be with me, because as soon as I saw something really neat or heard about some cool object or event from the past, I started seeing my characters doing or experiencing it. That was fine, except when I walked — totally centuries away from where I actually was — not paying attention to what I was doing. The other person's job was to stop me from walking into walls, or falling off cliffs, or stepping off curbs into traffic. When I sat down to write

These could be weapons of mass destruction! Captain Stella thought. *With the lightning speed of a finely tuned scientific mind, she made a decision.*
Diving from her place against the wall she hurled herself forward and grasped for the green bullet that was even then piercing through the air. It didn't matter that she herself could be mortally wounded. She couldn't let anyone else be hurt.

The bullet hit the palm of her hand, and she curled her fingers around it just as gravity pushed her to the floor. Even before she hit the ground she could feel the tiny green object giving way to a soft mush in her hand. It could be some form of biological warfare —

Or it could be a pea. Sophie sat on the floor, right at the feet of Julia Cummings and stared at her open palm. A green mass was squished right in the middle.

"Gross me out!" Julia said.

Ms. Quelling stood over Sophie, looking down between two thick curtains of bronze-colored hair.

"Sophie," she said. "*What on earth!*

(from *Sophie and the Scoundrels*)

those books, and the phone rang, I remember thinking, "What is that?" And it was like I had to come back several centuries or decades in order to answer it. I still find myself wondering how my characters are doing—then I realize that, if I want to know, I should sit down and write what happens next!

Why are Sophie and her sister totally different people?

There does tend to be an expectation that members of the same family should be the same or very similar. Sophie's father spends a lot of time not being able to understand why Sophie isn't like Lacie. I think that's something a lot of kids with siblings, especially superstar siblings, can relate to.

I drew on my relationship with my sister to write about Sophie and Lacie. Even though I was the younger one, I was the little shining star in my family, doing everything everyone told me to do absolutely perfectly. Phyllis was a little bit of a black sheep, following her own path. Even though Phyllis and my mother were more alike than my mother and I were, they fought a lot; while my mother and I hardly fought at all. Phyllis and I have always been very different. She was pretty—I was smart. She always loved boys. I was a slow bloomer when it came to the absurd little creeps. She cooked and sewed and did hair. I read and wrote and played the piano. She didn't let anybody walk on her. I turned myself inside out trying to make everybody happy. She taught me the things I never would have figured out—like how to shave my legs, ask a boy to a Sadie Hawkins dance, and make pizza from a box.

Isn't it amazing how two people with the same parents, who grow up in the same house at roughly the same time and are around each other all the time can be so completely different? It happens all the time, because God made each of us to be unique, and we respond to our childhood situations uniquely. The Sophie Series is about how to express yourself and be assertive when you're different, even if you're different from your own family. I wanted readers to see that you can love someone and even learn to live with them, despite the fact that you sometimes might feel like you—or they—are, like, from the planet Zorebon.

"We're all alike in the important things," Sophie said.

"Yes!" Darbie pulled her eyebrows together. "Tell us what they are, Sophie."

Sophie got up on her knees so she could look right into Maggie's dark, sad eyes. "None of us are perfect," she said. "But we ALL try to follow our rules—like we're all mostly loyal and we don't do bad stuff to people like the Corn Pops even though they do it to us—and we TRY to do the right thing. When we fight, we always make up because—"

Sophie stopped and slid her eyes toward Kitty—whose parents "didn't believe in church." She was pretty sure Jesus would want her to go ahead anyway.

"Because love is always where it starts with God."

Willoughby stuck her hand up. "If you call Julia and them Corn Pops," she said, "what do you call yourselves?"

Darbie and Fiona and Kitty whipped their heads toward Sophie.

"Willoughby totally helped us," Sophie said. "Of course we can tell her. We're the Corn Flakes."

Willoughby gave a nod that bounced her wavy bob. "Then I want to be one," she said.

(from *Sophie's First Dance?*)

Why do you have Fiona speak a little French?

Just to show that she's so smart and she likes knowing something new. There's a little piece of Fiona that likes to show off, but it's a good kind of showing off. There's nothing wrong with letting other people know that you're smart, or that you're creative, or even that you know French. One of the best things about Fiona as Sophie's friend is that she models for Sophie that it's okay to be yourself, even when other people don't understand what the Sam Hill you're talking about.

What book is your favorite?

Now that is like trying to pick a favorite child! I work really hard on all the books I write. They all have things about them I wish could be better, and they all have a special place in my heart. However, I can probably narrow it down a little bit more than that.

I really love *Lily and the Creep*, because I think that book is a turning point for Lily, when she really has to see somebody in a different way. That's also why I like *Lights, Action, Lily!* I truly love *Sophie's Stormy Summer*, because in that book, everything that Sophie has been learning about herself, and being a friend, and standing up for what's right comes into play in a really difficult situation. I was just so proud of her when I finished writing that book.

In real life, I really hate it when there's conflict—you know, fights and arguments and stuff. But when I write, what I really love is when there's tension, and low points, and internal struggles. I sure put those poor kids through a lot! Of course, it's nothing next to the Christian Heritage Series. Those poor kids are constantly in *physical* danger—getting shot at, hanging from planes, being tied up, bitten by snakes, and falling down mountains. But even in those books, my favorite parts were when the characters had to do something that was really hard for them emotionally, rather than physically, like tell the truth, ask for help, or be nice to someone who was being a general piece of dirt.

Did you model Sophie's friends after Lily's?

I try never to repeat characters from book to book or series to series, unless, of course, it actually is the same person. I keep all my characters' names on a list in a binder, so I can be sure I don't re-use names, and I try to develop even very minor characters as their own people. But I can see why someone would ask that, because sometimes people fill roles in our lives that are very similar.

It seems sometimes like there are types of girls, doesn't it? Bossy ones, shy ones, popular ones, smart ones. In both Lily and Sophie's groups of friends, there's a bossy friend, a shy friend, a quirky friend, a friend without much confidence, and a leader friend, who is Lily in the Lily books and Sophie in the Sophie books. I didn't do that on purpose, but in trying to make the girls within each series different from each other, it was helpful to have each fulfill a different role and then make them physically distinct from any other character. Then, as I write each book, each and every character, no matter how small his or her role in the book, just starts to take on a personality of his or her own. The role or type I cast them as is only a starting place.

Are you going to write another series like Sophie or Lily?

I am writing another series for eight- to twelve-year-old girls, but it's going to be a little different from Lily and Sophie. Her name is Lucy, and as big as some of Sophie and Lily's struggles have been, they really don't have anything on what this poor girl has been through. Sophie's and Lily's families have been pretty traditional — a mom, a dad, some siblings, house, cars, your basic middle school — but Lucy doesn't have a lot of those things. I'm also planning to write some nonfiction books that go along with these fiction books, but instead of dealing with topics like friends or your changing body, they will be guides to studying certain parts of the Bible by comparing it to your own experience, as this character will do in the fiction books.

So keep your eyes open for ... Lucy Rooney!

Will you please make a Lily/Sophie movie, and can I be in it?

I cannot tell you how many girls have asked me this question. Some of them have even sent pictures, resumes, or requests to make their own movies! It's sort of neat to see a book as a movie, isn't it? It's fun to compare the way you imagined something in your head to how a director made it come to life. Movies like *The Lion, the Witch, and the Wardrobe* are really impressive examples of what Hollywood can do, but even TV movies like the American Girl stories or *Anne of Green Gables* are fun to see. And, of course, we can always compare notes afterward about how *we* would have done it.

Keep in mind, though, that producing a movie takes A LOT of money. Just one roll of cinema film can cost thousands of dollars — that's if you have a camera. And what about costumes, props, and sets?

Are you starting to understand why I am not personally in

charge of getting my books made into movies? I promise if anyone ever approaches me and asks if they may make a movie about Sophie or Lily, and if they promise to do them justice and not leave the God stuff out, I will allow those movies to be made. But that's pretty much the extent of a writer's involvement in making a movie, unless he or she writes the script. Once it's in a filmmaker's hands, a book becomes that artist's creative project and starts being a new and different work of art.

As Sophie stared out the bus window and watched the signs on I-64 herald their approach to the Poquoson turnoff, she sank low enough to crawl under the seat. What had just happened?

She always came up with the ideas for their films.

She always dreamed up the main character and played her in the movie.

There had never been any question that *she* would direct.

After all, wasn't she the one who had gotten her own camera and started making films of her daydreams with just Fiona and then Maggie, and later Kitty, and then Willoughby?

If it wasn't for her, would there even be a Film Club? Would the Lucky Charms even have people to make amazing videos with?

There was only one thing to do, she decided as the bus pulled up in front of the school. That was to show her fellow Flakes and the Charms that they needed her to be in charge.

Because if she wasn't Sophie LaCroix, the great film director — who was she?

(from *Sophie Loses the Lead*)

Oh, and all you budding actresses out there, if Hollywood ever seeks me out, I'll point them in your direction.

Are you just so fascinated with Sophie and Lily that you can hardly stand it? Is it all totally leaking out your ears? You may remember, from chapter one, that when I got to feeling that way about my Nancy Drew books, I started to *write*. Wanna give it a try?

chapter three

The Write Stuff

Answers to Your Writing Questions

What advice would you give me to become a good writer like you?

There are three important parts to becoming a good writer:

- First, you have to **read**.
- Second, you have to **live**.
- And third, you have to **write**.

Reading books does a lot for your writing. Not only can it inspire you to be a writer and kick-start your imagination, but your brain stores away how sentences should be put together, when paragraphs should stop, and how stories are supposed to flow. Reading also improves your vocabulary, because you see words you might not recognize on their own in a context that helps them make sense. Seeing words over and over again while reading also helps improve your spelling.

But if you want to come up with your own stories, you also have to live — not as in maintaining a pulse and breathing in and out, but as in getting out and experiencing things. Even if you're home-schooled or only go into town once a week, you still interact with other people when you *do* go to town. And I bet you have siblings, parents, animals, a yard or a field or the woods, or people in your apartment complex, and a nearby city park, birds on your window-sill, whatever. The point is, you have to *live* these things to be a writer. You have to pay attention to them — what they sound like, look like, smell like, feel like, and mean to you. You have to get in there and participate — talk to people, feed the birds, run around in the field. If you want to have anything to write about, you have to have a life, and you have to get a bunch of it on you.

Then, if you want to be a writer, you have to write. And if you want to be a good writer, you have to write all the time. That's the only way it's going to happen. Some writers set quotas for them-selves, such as making sure they write a certain number of pages or words per day.

If you're going to be "good" at writing someday, you have to give yourself permission to maybe be a little bit bad at it at first. There are lots of starts out there that stop short of an entire book, or story, or even paragraph. But the important thing is to start any-way, and keep starting over and over again. When you were learn-ing to ride a bike or scooter, skate or do a cheer, did you get it perfect the very first time? Writing is the same way.

And not feeling like it, not feeling inspired, is not a reason for not writing. You have to sit down and write even if you don't think you can. Trust me, you can. Since I make my living as a writer, I have to show up at my desk every writing day. There are days when I would rather be shopping, or I have something nagging at my mind, or I have this little hangnail ... but I sit down and do my best. Some days it's hard to write, but there is always something worth keeping. The thing is — there certainly wouldn't be if I didn't write anything at all!

If you're one of those people who has perfectionist issues (like me), you might want to try keeping a journal that no one will ever read (including you) so you don't have to feel embarrassed about what you write. Or you can type things on the computer and delete them when you're done. Or if you save them, go back and reread them later to see how you've improved. Write on a roll of paper towels if you want to, but if you want to be a writer, then WRITE. Commit to it.

It can be a blast to combine these three steps: reading, living, and writing. Keep a journal about books you've read. Or keep a little notebook with you all the time and write down things you see and do. Or, visit a setting where a book takes place and do something that a character in the book did, and then write about that experience. These are all things I have done and sometimes still do. And it's worked for me.

How do you think of all those characters?

There are two kinds of writers: plot-driven writers and character-driven writers. I happen to be a character-driven writer, which means that the things going on inside my characters create the plots of my stories. They are what make things happen. For example, when Lily needed to learn what real beauty is, I put her in a situation where she became a model so she could learn that. Make sense?

Now, if the situation is what occurs to me first, pretty quickly I come up with a character to experience that situation, and imagine how that situation would affect him or her. I wanted to write about growing up in Williamsburg during the American Revolution, so I dreamed up Thomas Hutchinson of The Williamsburg Years (in The Christian Heritage Series). He had to be strong and grow up fast because there was a war going on around him.

For a while, as I'm planning a series, a character is just a person that I'm getting to know. I find pictures that look like the character I'm imagining, and I write in a journal in the voice of that person. (Yes, Sophie has a journal and Lucy has a book of lists—how fun is that?) And then it occurs to me that maybe that person has a mother, or a husband, or a girlfriend, or friends, whatever. And then those people start to take on shapes of their own. I find their pictures too. I usually dig through magazines and pull out advertisements, but sometimes I meet someone who looks like my character and ask if I can take their picture. I write snippets about them in a big binder; and while I'm doing dishes or walking Captain and Sully (they're my dogs, remember—very helpful with writing) or sitting in doctors' waiting rooms, I think about how those characters act when they're around my main character. That's because all my characters have to grow out of the main character. They're the people he or she has to run into and get to know in order to experience growth as a person and finish the story.

Whichever kind of writer an author happens to be, I guarantee you that all writers pull from their own experience to flesh out the people in their books. Maybe it's your beloved grandmother, or maybe it's someone you saw on the beach doing something really outlandish and never saw again. But if it sticks in your mind, it may end up in a book.

Where do you get your characters' names?

When I was teaching, I got a lot of characters' names from my students, especially last names, because there were some kids with surnames not even I could have come up with out of thin air. Krewdel, Hauseladen, and Schifferdecker (that last one was actually a teacher) were some of my favorites. But for first names, if something doesn't occur to me right off the bat, I refer to a book of baby names I keep in my desk drawer. The phone book is great for last names.

For every book I write, I make a binder. In every binder I keep a copy of the contract for that book, the plot summary and outline, and dividers, making a section for each character. I glue the pictures I cut out for the characters onto the dividers. In the sections I write down physical characteristics, notes about the characters' pasts, and anything that helps me develop each of them. Toward the front of every binder I keep a sheet of paper with the alphabet on it, A–Z down the margin. I write the name of the character that starts with each letter next to the letter it starts with—Sarah with S, Jimmy with J—and that way I can make sure I don't have any characters who have names starting with the same letter, unless I do it on purpose. I might do it with twins or with characters the main character tends to mix up with one another. I think it's confusing when characters in a book have similar names to other characters in the same book, which is why I try not to let that happen. I also try to avoid having characters with the same names as characters in other series. It's a good thing there are, like, millions of names in the world. Choosing names is one of the most fun parts of fiction, especially when I can match the name to the personality. (Think about Xavier Wormley, a character in The Williamsburg Years. Guess what kind of guy he was!)

Where do you get your ideas for stories (names, personalities, settings, obstacles for the characters, and conflicts)?

Lots of writers would tell you, "Write what you know." Now, that is not the same thing as "only write about things that have happened to you in the real world," "only write about places you have .

physically been to," or "only write about realistic things." If that were the case, we would have no Narnia, no Middle Earth, no stories about the past, no stories about the future ... we would have no fiction of any kind. "Write what you know" means that at the core of what you're writing about, there has to be something that is real to you, or it won't be real to your readers.

For example, I'm not a redheaded eleven-year-old, but I am a go-get-'em kind of person, so at the core of the Lily character, there is a person I can relate to and represent from my own experience. I am also not a shy, day-dreamy twelve-year-old, but my daughter was, so I could represent Sophie from my own experience. I don't live in a house on the beach, but I've stayed in a house on the beach, so I can tell other people what it's like. I wasn't alive in the 1690s (although I have enough gray hairs to look like I was!), but after reading dozens of nonfiction books about what life was like in the 1690s, going into houses that still look the way they did in the 1690s, seeing clothes worn by people in the 1690s, and reading books that actually were written in the 1690s; that time period became something I *had* experienced, and understood, so I could show that experience to others. Besides, it wasn't the clothes and houses and stuff of the 1690s that were important in the books I wrote about the Salem years, but rather things like being left out or excluded from society, justice, and just plain growing up. That's how I could write about them.

I get a bunch of my ideas from my friends and family. Some come from movies, TV, books and magazine articles. Other ideas pop up from random things that happen at the table next to mine in a restaurant or two rows over on an airplane. Some come my way from other people, like readers who send me letters or folks I meet when I travel and teach and speak. Still others appear from my life—stuff that's happened to me and stuff that I've missed out on too.

The cool thing about ideas is that once you have one, if you feed it a little, give it a little imagination, a little room to stretch out, it will start producing other ideas faster than those Tribble things on Star Trek (again, ask your parents). Sometimes ideas come from other ideas. And sometimes ideas come out of nowhere, when you're not even looking. I like to think that those ideas come as Express Mail, straight from God.

How do you get so many interesting ideas in all of your books?

I need to break this question down into two sections — the "how do you get them in" part and the "interesting" part.

All stories — short, long, and where-are-the-CliffsNotes long — have the same structure: beginning, middle, and end. And what makes the difference in the length is, very simply, how much extra stuff you pack in. If you have only seven pages to say what you want to say — and sometimes in school or when you're writing for a magazine you are going to have really tight limits like this — then you have to be really picky about what you're going to include. So when you're introducing your heroine, for example, you might just say, "Sue had long, brown hair." Now, if you were writing a book about the same length as one of my Lily or Sophie books, you might say, "Sue had long, chestnut brown hair that she wore in braids that hung down her back like two, shiny ropes." And if you were going hog-wild and writing something WAY long, you might write, "The young woman who entered the room was named Sue. She had long, glistening hair, the color of chestnut mares standing in the noonday sun, and it hung down her back in perfect plaits that swung with her every step like ropes that swing from the gallows."

In order to give length to a story, you've got to put in many ideas — which brings me to the "interesting" part.

I have another phrase that I use instead of interesting, and that is "delicious." When I am writing—and when I teach other people about writing—I say, "You have to make it delicious." You need details that appeal to people's five senses. Readers need to be able to see, hear, smell, taste, and touch your story in order to be truly captivated by it. THAT is what makes it "interesting."

No cases had been brought before them yet, and Sophie was anxious for one. It would be a great opportunity to be like Liberty Lawhead—

Who entered the room with her jaw set, looking down from her impressive height into the eyes of a heinous offender who had stomped on the rights of an innocent person. He looked back at her, his face set with stubborn heinous-ness, but she met his gaze firmly, without wavering. He finally dropped his gaze. He had obviously seen the honor in her eyes, honor he could never hope to match—

"What are you looking at?"

Sophie found herself blinking into an unfamiliar face. Hazel eyes, set close to a straight, very-there nose, blinked back at her. The girl shook sandy-blonde bangs away from her eyebrows and pulled back her upper lip. Sophie wasn't sure it was a smile, but she couldn't take her eyes off the gap between the girl's two front teeth.

(from *Sophie Tracks a Thief*)

Do you always write the chapters in order?

Yes.

No, seriously—when I write a book, before I actually start all the juicy descriptions and fun stuff, I first plan out absolutely every single thing that's going to happen. It's called an outline. I decide how many chapters there are going to be, what's going to happen in each one, and how the book's going to end. Then I start at the beginning and work straight through. Otherwise, I would never have finished a single book.

Not all authors do this. Some people find it easier to start at the middle or end of the story—whatever part is clearest in their heads, and then build out from there. Every writer has to find out what works best for him or her. I've always been the super-organized-control-weenie type, so having an outline and writing from it works best for me. Then I don't have to keep going back and making sure everything is consistent and all the loose ends are tied up, because I tie them as I go.

Are you ever shy about your books, like you don't want people to see what you've written?

If you want to get paid to write, you have to put yourself out there and know that even if your writing gets rejected, that doesn't mean you're a bad writer. It just means you need to keep trying. It could also mean that piece of writing didn't happen to be right for that magazine or publisher.

Having said that, when you are just starting out and not yet trying to pay all the bills with your next book deal, and your stuff probably isn't the next number one on the New York Times

Bestseller List, you should be careful who you show it to. It's nice to get other people's opinions and support, but some people think they're helping when they are actually, you know, ripping your heart out. Not literally, but when people say things like, "Well, this part is bad," or "You really need to work on your spelling—no one's going to be able to understand this!" it can really hurt. It can also discourage you from writing. So while you're still developing your craft, it's better to show your stuff to people you trust to be as encouraging as they are editorial.

> I love to write, but when I start a story, the next day I get new ideas that won't fit in the story I'm writing. So I have to start a new one. So every day, I'm writing a new story and I can never work on the others because I'm always getting new ideas! What do you do when you get new ideas?

It's really normal, when you first start writing, not to complete everything you start. Not everything has to be finished. Writing for the sake of writing is more the point right at first. However, when you're on idea overflow like this girl, it might be time to take evasive action.

Instead of starting a new story every time an idea occurs to you, try jotting that idea down in a special idea notebook, then continue to work on the story you were writing the day before. (That's what I do.) When that one's finished, you can get out your idea book and see which idea appeals to you to write about next. You also might find a way to incorporate your new idea into the current story you're working on. Or just keep starting a new story every day. Work on more than one story per day. Eventually, there's going to be a story that you can't NOT finish.

After you finish writing a book but before you send it in to the editor, what process do you go through with the book to get it ready?

Well, first I run spell check. I have got to say, that is the best thing ever invented. I can spell when I put my mind to it, but when I'm cranking out a chapter or more a day, I don't stop to make sure my i's are dotted and my t's are crossed. After spell check, I read through quickly to make sure everything makes sense, I didn't leave anything out, and words like "than" that should be "that" get changed.

Then I read it one last time, and pretend I'm eleven again. It can be as correct as correct can be, but if it isn't really a good book that girls are going to enjoy, who cares? If eleven-year-old Nancy likes it, then I attach the whole thing to an email and send it to my editor with a line in the email like, "Here it is! Oh boy!"

What were some of your favorite writing experiences?

For me, writing is so much about the work I do before I ever sit down at the computer. My favorite writing experiences are usually the times when I'm out "getting it on me," especially when other people are willing to play along. One of my favorite times was when we went to Williamsburg in November, and it was REALLY cold. We took a carriage ride, and the driver stopped and picked up another passenger, the Widow *somebody*—I don't remember her name. Anyway, she was so cool. She told us all the gossip about everyone alive in that town in 1790, or whenever. We were just howling. She wore a big dress and a wool cape, and her hands were in the most beautiful leather mitts. The horse was clip-clopping along, and outside it was getting dark and all the lanterns were lit. When I had to write scenes like that in the books about the Williamsburg years, I could close my eyes and feel the sway of the carriage and the raw cold on my cheeks and nose, and smell the oiled leather of the seats and the tack on the horses.

Do you ever get really excited about the events of the books you're writing?

Oh yeah, definitely. Because I do so much prep work before I sit down to write, when I am at the computer, I feel like there's a movie playing inside my head, and I'm trying to get it all down on the page as it's playing. So when characters are running away or having an argument or solving the mystery, it's like it's really happening for me in that moment.

Marijean likes to tell the story about finding me at my computer at 5:00 a.m. on a day in January. She and I were supposed to leave to do research for the Chicago series (talk about "getting it on you"—we fell in the iciest puddle of water you can possibly imagine while we were there—but that's another story!). I had to turn in the last book of the Charleston years before we left, so I'd been up all night finishing it. I was writing about Austin and his family escaping while Lottie rode by on her horse. She was trying to divert the men chasing them, so all she could do to say good-bye was wave. I'm sobbing, and Marijean comes out in her pajamas and says, "Mom, what is going on with you right now?" And I said, "They didn't even get to say good-bye!" Four hours later we were in Chicago, and, needless to say, the first thing we did was put me down for a nap. But yes, I get pretty into it.

How did you really get inspired to write?

If you really want to write, I think—no, I *believe*—that what is inspiring you is God. I think God made me to be a writer, giving me the kind of mind and soul that could turn my experiences into stories to share with others. And all the time I think God's been there, whispering (or sometimes screaming, depending on whether or not I'm paying attention) "Go for it, Nance—write, write, write, write, go, go, GO!" I think of God as a creative force that wants us, his creations, to realize our fullest potential. For those of us created to be writers, that means writing. So when I get a little plot idea or feel a nagging that says, "I could so write a better book than that," that's God, baby. If you feel that nagging, don't ignore it. After all, I won't be around to write forever. Somebody has to do it—why not you?

chapter four

God's Bod

Answers to Your Body Questions

What if I get too much makeup on and I can't get it all off — what do I do?

First of all, don't panic! Your skin is not an eternal, permanent substance, and makeup is not oil-based paint. Even if you do manage to get something on your face that doesn't come off with a good wash with soap and water, human skin is a membrane made of three main layers, each one made up of even more layers than that (freaky weird, huh?). The top layers, which are about as deep as your makeup is going to sink, are constantly dying, flaking off, and being replaced by new skin. So even if your L'Oréal seems resistant to everything including coarse grit sandpaper, it's coming off eventually, I guarantee it.

By the way, uh, don't use coarse grit sandpaper on your face!

However, makeup can be difficult to get off, especially now that most companies have long-lasting varieties of mascara, lipstick, blush, and foundation. I think the worst two things to try and wash off are waterproof mascara and long-lasting lipstick. Obviously something made to resist water is not coming off just because you splash a little tap water in its direction. Soap helps, but a soap with a moisturizer in it works better than normal soap. Also, try applying some lotion or petroleum jelly or even a little olive or sesame oil to your eyelids and lips before you wash. It will lubricate the little adhesive substances in the cosmetics and make them come off easier, and it will do it without making your skin all raw from scrubbing.

If you don't have super-sensitive skin, and you're really having trouble removing something, you could try a facial scrub. You can buy them at the grocery store — everything from really expensive microbeads to not-so-expensive apricot scrub — or you could make one at home with little oatmeal and yogurt. Put about 1/4 cup uncooked oatmeal in the food processor. Chop it fine. Then put it in a bowl and mix it with a little bit of yogurt; not in the blender. Take your mixture to the bathroom and stand over the sink, wearing your grubby clothes or covering yourself (but NOT with your mother's best towels). Spread the oatmeal scrub all over your face. Rub it around for a minute or two, and then rinse your face with cold water. This works for every skin type, even sensitive, and it moisturizes and exfoliates (removes layers of dead skin).

I have fine hair. How do I take care of my hair?

I know a lot about fine hair. It means that each individual hair is thin and soft, and you may have fewer hair follicles on your scalp than the girl who sits next to you in class who looks like she has enough hair to share with 37 people. If your hair seems to completely disappear in size when you braid it or put it in a ponytail … if it ties itself into knots every time you turn your head … if it doesn't take curl from a curling iron or hot rollers well … or if it naturally wants to hang as close to your scalp as it possibly can, you might have fine hair—like me and Marijean, whose hair was entrusted to my care for the first ten years of her life.

Anyway, the trick with fine hair is not to expect too much from it. You've got to keep it clean, of course, and use a conditioner for detangling and moisturizing. Comb it out when it's wet with a wide-toothed comb, and when it's dry, you should use a soft-bristled paddle brush. If you want to try to curl your hair or make it look fluffy and full, you're going to need what my niece Heather, uber-beauty queen, calls "product"—mousses, gels, and hairspray. Put in mousse when it's wet, blow-dry it from underneath with your head hanging upside down. If you have short hair, you can then add gel and style, like I do, or you can skip the gel and go for the hot-curling implements. After you've curled and gotten your hair into whatever position you want it in, you can spray it with hairspray. I encourage you to use something besides aerosol. It's really not good for the environment.

Of course, every product and every source of heat you apply to your hair, including blow-dryers, damages it some. It dries it out and makes it brittle, or easily breakable. All that stuff also makes your hair less soft and not as shiny. If you just do the curlers and the blow-dryer once in a while—when you want to feel special or look extra nice—it's not going to permanently suck all the life from your hair. But if you do it every day, you have to start playing catch-up with all the products out there that promise to repair your hair.

So moisturizing shampoos and conditioners, air-drying, and a good, thorough brushing with a soft-bristled paddle brush is the best way to care for fine hair. Marijean looks for products that have rosemary in them. Sometimes she takes a bunch of rosemary, the spice, from the kitchen (she says about two tablespoons) and soaks it in a cup of hot water. When the water cools, she strains out the rosemary and takes the water into the shower. After she rinses out her shampoo and conditioner, she pours the rosemary water over her hair and rubs it in, like a rinse. She says it makes her hair shiny. I would have to agree!

I'm Nigerian, so I have really short hair, and that bothers me because all my cousins have longer hair than I do. What can I do about this?

There are lots of people whose hair just won't grow long—it just *won't*. It's a genetic thing (you know, you're born that way), and it happens all over the world to people of all races. Marijean's friend, Mairin (see the fire story in chapter two) has blonde hair that won't grow past her shoulders no matter what she does. Some people have hair that curls really tightly, and if they grow it long, it becomes a big cloud of poofiness. Some people go ahead and grow it out, and it looks great, and some people hate the way it looks.

If you are comparing yourself to your cousins or friends or sisters or even the covers at the magazine rack, you should STOP and look for the beauty inside yourself. It is not conceited or vain to find things to appreciate about you. It is not wrong to feel good about the way you look. And the way that you look is also not all that you are. Every single person on this earth is a combination of the internal and the external. The external has its uses and its fun and its everyday part in our lives, but the internal is so, so, so much more powerful and important. The external lets you express who you are inside, with how you dress and what you look like. Who you are inside is always beautiful, as long as it's your authentic self. So however that comes out—through your style of dress, your healthy hair and skin, your smile or your tears—is gorgeous. Your cousins and your mom and your friends are beautiful too. It's not a competition anyway!

I want to color my hair — I just want to try something different. My dad says I can't because that's changing the way God made me. But he shaves his face, and my mom shaves her legs, and I'm allowed to <u>cut</u> my hair — isn't that changing the way God made you? Why should God care if I color my hair?

This is a really tough question. There is so much going on here!

If you want to dye your hair because you think you look ugly, or because you want to fit in, or because you don't want to look like a nerd, or any other reason that falls into the slightly misguided category, then I don't think it's a good idea. Changing your outside doesn't change your inside — it's the other way around. The *inside* is the part God cares about. When the outside is more important to you than the inside, I think God may be thinking, "Hmm, let's rethink that, shall we?"

Okay, now let's look at the parent issue here. I don't know exactly why your dad is saying no, but I can imagine lots of reasons beyond not wanting to change the way God made you. Maybe your dad thinks you're too young, or maybe he thinks trying to be cool like some other girl with colored hair at your school isn't a good reason. Maybe your family can't afford to have your hair dyed. Maybe your dad thinks the chemicals will be bad for you. If this is an important issue for you, talk to your parents about the choices you want to make about your body and find out what their real reasons are. We really can't ignore the whole "honor thy parents" thing, girls. It's in the Ten Commandments, and besides that, it's usually not such a bad idea, even when it's frustrating, even when it seems lame.

Parents don't have all the right answers all the time. They're human beings, and they don't know everything. But it's possible their years of experience may have increased their wisdom a little bit, and they most certainly love you and want your life to be easier, not harder, than their lives were when they were kids.

"You have such a cute figure, Lacie," Aunt Bailey said as she gave the tape measure a professional snap. "I don't think the bras you're wearing are showing it off at all."

"I think the bras she's wearing are just fine," Mama said. Her elfin lips were tight. They reminded Sophie of the top of a drawstring bag.

"Let me treat the girl to a nice foundation garment or two." Aunt Bailey suddenly swept her eyes, bright blue in her colored contacts, over Sophie. "I would buy Sophie some too, but I don't see any signs of development there at all."

Sophie crossed her arms over her chest and felt her face going BEYOND scarlet.

"She's a late bloomer," Mama said. She put her arm around Sophie's shoulders.

"Still," Aunt Bailey said. She tilted her head, its hair gelled into a dozen auburn flips, and gave Sophie a thorough going over with her eyes. "She could use a little padded bra. That would be cute."

"No!" Sophie said. "I'm not gonna pretend I have breasts when I don't!"

"Why not?" Lacie said. "You pretend everything else."

(from *Sophie's Secret*)

I'm really fat. My whole class says so, plus I don't wear the same size as any of my friends. I hate it. What should I do about this?

The mother in me just wants to march into your classroom and start lecturing. I don't care if you weigh 300 pounds and have ten heads — NO ONE has the right to tell you who you are or make you feel like less than you are. I don't happen to remember God saying "Thou shalt not gain weight," nor do I recall, "Blessed are the thin-waisted, calorie-counting gym bunnies." Puh-leeeeze! "Fat" people can be absolutely beautiful physically, and "fat" people can be wonderful, beautiful people internally. But how thin or fat you are is never, never, NEVER a factor in your value as a person.

Now I do admit that there is an obesity problem in America. There are a lot of overweight kids out there, most of whom have overweight parents. This is concerning because being overweight can increase the risk of all kinds of health problems, like diabetes, heart disease, cancer, and arthritis. If you really are "fat," I am concerned about your health and the health of all girls like you. That includes mental and emotional health.

But none of that changes the FACT that every person is worth as much as the next person, because every person is made by God. I know *not* comparing yourself to others is hard, especially if they are comparing you to themselves too. If you're in a situation like this, here's what I suggest:

First off, if people are giving you a hard time, draw the line. DO NOT put up with people making fun of you or saying nasty things about you. Tell them to stop, and then tell a teacher about the situation. Worried about being unpopular or having those people mad at you? Um, why do you want them to like you? Why do you care what they think, when they already obviously think of you as a punching bag? You need to assert your right to not be picked on. Mobilize your teachers, your parents, and any friends your age who are *real* friends, people who don't care what your jeans size is and don't say horrible things about you. It's not going to be easy, but if you're not going to do it for you, do it because God wants you to. That's right — God made you and loves you and wants you to be happy, and being happy includes protecting yourself.

Second, if you're going to stop comparing yourself to others, you're going to need something to compare yourself to. No, seriously. You can't take away something and not put something else in its place and expect that the first thing won't come right back. You, sister, need a new gauge, a new yardstick, and that yardstick is YOU. You need to find out the numbers that really matter and start looking at those. In order to find out, you need to turn to someone who knows what he or she is talking about, and in this case, that is certainly not Miss Sixth Grade Vogue Editor, or Mr. Junior High Beauty Contest Judge. It isn't even your parents, unless one of them happens to be a doctor.

That's right — go to a doctor. Every single person's body is different. We mature at slightly different times, gain and lose weight differently, grow to different heights, etc. A doctor can take a look at you and tell you what you, if you were in perfect health, should weigh. That doctor can also tell you what your blood pressure should be, what your cholesterol should be, and how much exercise and sleep you should be getting. When you find out what's normal, as in, what's the best you that you can be right now, you can start comparing yourself to and making changes to be that. Here are some numbers to get you started:

30 The number of minutes a day you should be getting cardiovascular exercise—that's exercise that gets your heart really pumping.

8 The number of hours you should be sleeping at night; nine or ten is even better.

5 The number of servings of fresh vegetables and fruits you should be eating per day. A serving is about the size of the palm of your hand.

3 The number of servings of low-fat dairy and whole grains (like oatmeal or whole wheat bread) you should be eating a day.

0 The number of times you should listen to what other people think about you.

You know whether or not you're a good person inside. And if you keep showing it, the right kind of people will see it. Those are the people you should hang out with. If you're not the same size as they are, well, you'll never have to worry about them borrowing your clothes and messing them up. And that is a huge wardrobe benefit!

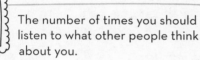 *All my friends have their ears pierced, and I don't. I feel like a baby, but I don't want pierced ears, really. I'm afraid it will hurt and that earrings will get caught on stuff. What if they rip out of my ears!?!?*

There is no universal law that says you have to get your ears pierced. We all want to do things at different times, and we may not do some things at all because they're not our thing, and, once again, *that's okay.*

I know women whose mothers had them get their ears pierced when they were little, and they let the holes close when they grew up because they didn't want to take the time to pick out earrings every morning. I know women who love earrings and have more than one hole in each ear so they can wear all of their earrings. I know women who wear the same pair of earrings almost every day and never take them off. It's up to you when the time is right—that is, unless your mom and dad have forbidden it.

It does hurt a little bit to get your ears pierced. There is a tiny prick at the time, and then your earlobes are a little sore afterward—which makes sense because someone just punched holes in them. The anxiety leading up to the actual piercing is a lot worse than the pain—trust me. But not wanting to do something purely cosmetic to yourself because it might hurt is a totally legitimate reason not to do it. I'm sure not going to wax my legs, I can tell you. I know women who swear by it. It's so great, they say. They hate shaving so much. But I am NOT pouring hot wax on myself, waiting for it to dry, then RIPPING it off along with all of my leg hair. No thank you!

And with everything else that we have to worry about as young women, let's not put comparing earlobes on the list, mmm-kay?

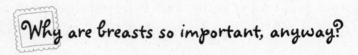

Why are breasts so important, anyway?

It sure does seem like breasts are a big deal, doesn't it? There is nothing wrong with breasts. They are a part of us, whatever shape or size they happen to be. They are there because they're part of the whole having-children thing. Like lots of other animals who breathe air and grow hair, female humans produce milk after they give birth so they have something to feed their babies. Before the invention of baby formula, the whole human race would have gone down the tubes without breasts. They are really just a biological thing. So what *is* the big deal?

It has to do with men. At a certain point in their lives, most male members of the human species stop picking their noses and rolling in the dirt (at least, all the time), and get interested in girls. Without this mysterious shift caused by hormones, the human species would never reproduce. Hormones are chemicals in the female body that tell it to grow breasts, cry for no apparent reason, and like boys. In the male body hormones tell it to do things like get hairy and smelly and, at the same time, try to get closer to girls — yeah, hormones don't really make a lot of sense all the time. And for some reason, when boys start noticing girls and wanting to be around them, the one thing they notice a whole lot is breasts. Maybe it's because they don't have them. Maybe it's because, somewhere deep in their brains, they kind of know that breasts have something to do with making sure the human race continues. I don't really have any idea. But boys, while in the process of becoming men, do get fixated on breasts.

When your breasts show up — whatever type of breasts they turn out to be — let yourself feel a little satisfaction that you just naturally, without even trying, have something so special that an entire half of our species wants it. This means that you also have something very precious that deserves to be protected and treated with respect — by you and everyone around you. It's a good thing to think about when you're picking out clothes. You get the idea.

I hate being tall. I'm the tallest person in my class — not girl, PERSON. I try to make myself shorter. I kind of lean to the side when I stand next to people. I'm almost as tall as my mom, and I'm twelve. What's your advice on this?

$\mathcal{M}$y advice is that you stand up straight. I was the tallest person — not girl, PERSON — in my class for years.

Yes, towering over boys at the age when everyone's starting to get interested in each other really, really stinks. You feel clumsy and no clothes fit right on you and you start to resent all those cute little, short girls. You slouch, you lean to the side, you tuck your shoulders in toward your chest, you round your spine ...

If you continue to try and hide your height, your shoulders and back are going to permanently curve inward. And when you reach your thirties, you may not be able to stand up straight all the way without some serious, painful effort. If you don't make that effort then, you won't be able to do it at all when you reach your fifties. How do I know? It happened to me. Let me tell you, the physical therapy I did to correct the slouching and hunching I did as a kid was really expensive, and it was HARD. If I could go back in time, I would tell myself to stand up straight!

Maybe you feel like you stick out. Why is that bad? Why do we always feel like we need to fit in and look like everyone else? We are not herd animals, my loves. We are not zebras. Lions are not on their way to pick us off. Sure, there will be people who ask you, "So how's the weather up there?" They may seem like lions right now, but they're actually just buzzards. They're the creatures who circle around looking for someone to pick on because they don't know any other way to make themselves feel okay. And that's just really sad.

So stand up. Walk tall! Use your height to express who you are, to show that you're confident and happy and fun. If you feel like a giraffe, well, be the best giraffe you can be. I guarantee that there are other giraffes out there — and maybe some monkeys, zebras, and cheetahs that don't mind looking up to you.

"Lilliputian," Dad said, "is a reference to the book *Gulliver's Travels*."

They all looked blankly at Dad.

"What's he talking about?" Art said to Mom.

"Joe asked why I call Lily 'Lilliputian.' It's a literary allusion."

"Great. Pass the salad," Art said.

"In the land of the Lilliputians," Dad went on, "Gulliver found the people to be extremely small."

"Then I still don't get why you call *her* that," Joe said. "Lily's, like, way tall."

"She's a beanpole," Art said. "What do I have to do to get the salad around here?"

"You have to stop being rude," Lily said. "And I am not a beanpole."

"What *is* a beanpole, anyway?" Joe asked. "I don't get that."

"Something tall and thin like your sister," Mom said. "Elbows, Joe."

Joe removed his elbows from the table and smiled at Lily like a little imp. "Does it have a big mouth?"

Lily gritted her teeth.

"Did he just ask if a beanpole has a mouth?" Dad asked, blinking behind his glasses.

Mom's lips twitched. "It isn't that Lily's mouth is so big. It's just that her face is so small."

Art stopped pouring ranch dressing onto his salad to look at Lily. "Nah," he said. "Her mouth's just big."

"Mo-om!" Lily said.

(from *Here's Lily!*)

I am so never going to get my period. Every other girl in my sixth-grade class has gotten it. I am so embarrassed!

Unless you have some kind of undiagnosed medical condition, you are probably going to get your period before you are fifteen. If you're really, really worried about it, you and your mom can find a doctor who can address this issue for you.

But if you're eleven, and you are thin or small for your age, your body just isn't at that place yet. Remember, your period starts when your body is at a physical place where it could, technically, be pregnant. It has to be physically strong enough and have the right hormones working before it could develop and carry another person around inside it for nine months. Look in the mirror—I'm serious—and ask yourself if your body looks like it could be carrying a baby around. If not, that's probably why you haven't had your period yet.

Now, moving on to the second half of your statement ... Does EVERY girl in your sixth-grade class really have her period? I am willing to positively guarantee that isn't the case. And if it were really true, well, so what? I know you can feel left out when a lot of people you hang around with are experiencing something and you're not, but there really isn't anything to be embarrassed about. It isn't because of anything you're doing or not doing.

You have a couple of options. First, you can choose not to tell people what your period status is and ask them not to talk about it around you. Real friends will respect this, even if you have to repeat yourself a couple of times. Second, you can take this opportunity to learn from the other girls, to get prepared for when it is your turn. What products do they use? What do they do when they have leaks? Were they prepared for their first time? Do they have a cute little bag or case to carry stuff around in?

What? Leaks? Products?!?!?! Yeah, it's not sounding like so much fun anymore, is it? But it's actually exciting when this transition happens in your life. It's a very special time. I think it's great to anticipate it, but don't beat yourself up by telling yourself there's something wrong with you if it hasn't happened yet. Each one of us is created individually, uniquely — differently. Yes, even in the period department.

I'm in fourth grade, and I started my period months ago. It's so embarrassing — I'm the only girl in my whole grade to have her period. I have to keep getting up to go to the bathroom, and everyone knows why. Is there anything I can do about this? What do you think?

Though there are plenty of girls who don't get their periods until they're thirteen or fourteen, lots of other girls are starting to get their periods as young as eight. There are many reasons for this — all completely out of your control. And yet, being the first person you know in your age group to start going through major physical changes can feel isolating and scary.

Try not to feel embarrassed. You didn't make your period start, and there's nothing wrong with your period starting no matter when or how or why it did. This is a natural thing that you can't control. As for people knowing why you are going to the bathroom, it's possible that people might notice that you're going more often or even wonder why. But unless you've told people why you're going to the bathroom, they probably don't know.

You can't make your period stop, and you can't control what other people think and do. But here are some things you can do. First, get prepared. Make sure you always have the stuff you need. The book *Body Talk* tells you everything you need to know about "the stuff." Put it in a special pouch in your backpack that isn't

"Ashley Adamson started her period!"

"No, she did not!" Reni said.

Suzy gave her little nervous giggle. "How do you know, Zooey?"

"I was in the bathroom when she found it," Zooey said, looking very important. "She came out of the stall all crying and saying, 'Chelsea—I started! What do I do!'"

"Ashley was actually crying?" Lily said.

"I would be too," Reni said. "That whole period thing is gross. I don't ever want to start mine."

"Is it gross, really?" Zooey said. "Is it, Lily?"

Lily chewed the inside of her mouth and said, "I don't know. I haven't gotten mine yet either."

"Whew," Suzy said, giggling, of course. "I thought I was the only one."

"Who cares?" Reni said. "I'll wait as long as God lets me before I have to start wearing those evil-looking pads and worrying about getting stuff on the seat of my desk—"

"When I start mine," Zooey said, "I don't want anybody else to know."

"Nobody will," Suzy said. And then her voice clouded over. "Will they?"

(from *Lily Robbins, M.D.*)

attached to your backpack — something that closes with a zipper or a snap. If you have your period while you're in school, take it out of your backpack in the morning and put it in your desk.

Second, make sure you have dark-colored clothes, especially pants, to wear to school on the days you have your period. Wear clothes that are also really comfortable so that the extra padding you have to deal with doesn't bother you so much (tighter jeans are out at this point in the month). That way, if you do have leaks (or think you do) they won't show, and you can totally cross that off your list of things to think about.

Third, you need allies. That first ally has to be your teacher. I KNOW the last thing you want to do is talk to your teacher about this, especially if your teacher is a man. But these are grown-ups, grown-ups who work with kids, no less, so they better be able to be sensitive about this kind of stuff. If your teacher knows what's going on, he or she can let you go to the bathroom without making a fuss. If you really, really, REALLY do not want to talk to your teacher, have your mom write you a note. It will totally make your life easier.

Another great ally for you is your mom, who has obviously been through this or you would not exist. She can offer all kinds of tips and tricks. Your friends can help too. So what if they don't have their periods yet? If you can trust them to keep your secret, you are now in a position to share your knowledge and experience with them. They will thank you for it! When you're there at the right moment with the maxi pad, stain remover, or the piece of chocolate, they'll love you for it and respect you. And they should, because you're being a great friend.

So really, this whole thing isn't some kind of solitary confinement punishment — it's actually an opportunity to be the wise, confident, good person I know you are. And I know God gave you this opportunity because you were the kind of young woman who could make the most of it.

chapter five

You Can't Live with 'em, You Can't Live without 'em

Answers to Questions about Friends and (Gasp!) Boys

What if I had a birthday party and no one showed up? What should I do?

That's one of those things that's probably *not* going to happen in real life. Still, it would be horrible, wouldn't it? Ergh.

If you send out invitations and everyone you want to invite actually receives one *and* you put the right date and time on the invitation, and *still* no one shows up, the first thing I would suggest is have a big ol' party for your own self. Hey, you've got balloons, streamers, cake, and ice cream—go for it! No matter what other people think or do, you should celebrate that you were born, because it's a good thing to be alive. And if you also need to have a good cry—hopefully in the arms of your very sympathetic mom or dad—just work that into the festivities. Got a piñata? Whack the candy right out of it, baby, and into the neighbor's yard three houses down.

Even if every single person who didn't come called and had a good reason for not attending, like loss of a limb or scarlet fever, you would still have the right to feel sad and disappointed. And if there were no phone calls, you'd have the right to feel hurt.

Then there's going to be the aftermath — when you run into all these people at school or church. You may WANT to tell these people to flush themselves down the toilet. It's okay to FEEL like doing that, but this would be one of those situations where you have to be what adults like to call "the bigger person." The "bigger" does not refer to your physical size, but rather to your heart, your brain, and your capacity for patience and forgiveness.

When you run into these people, don't pretend nothing happened (even if they do). Be honest. If you tell your friend how you feel, and if she reacts with actual remorse — really knows she's messed up and truly does feel bad about it — even though you're hurt, it's up to you to forgive her to her face for messing up. You have to repair your relationship by saying something along the lines of "You did hurt my feelings, but I know you didn't mean to, and I know you're really sorry. I forgive you, and I still want to be your friend."

If your friend does the really fakey, "Oh my gosh! I had no idea! How terrible! I'm, like, so sorry!" and you're pretty sure she doesn't mean it, keep being honest. Press her a little bit and tell her again that it really hurt your feelings. If she still doesn't seem to get it, I'm sorry to say, she's not the best friend in the world.

You don't have to say, "I forgive you" to her face, but you should let it go. Forgiving someone doesn't mean spending every spare minute with that person and letting them do whatever they want. It means you let go of your own pain without waiting for the other person to make it go away.

Finally, if your friend responds by acknowledging pretty matter-of-factly that she hurt you and couldn't give two straws, she is not your friend. If she's getting some kind of satisfaction out of hurting your feelings, she's a bully, and she's to be avoided at all costs.

Don't bare your feelings to her again — there's no point. Stay away from her, protect yourself from her, and don't give her the time of day. BUT ... forgive her. Yes, even her. Give it all up to God. You don't have to, and shouldn't, forgive her to her face — she may try to use it to hurt you again in some way. But in your heart, you need to.

Whew! That was one emotional birthday party! Isn't it interesting that we sometimes have these dark, nightmarish fantasies, these ideas that no one is going to like us? I think it just goes to show how scary it is to put yourself out there and try to be friends with someone else. That is why I put this question first in this chapter. Relationships with other people are a big deal, especially at the tween time in your life.

I have lots of friends, but I'm not sure they're real friends. Can you help me on that?

I sure can! If you have a really large group of friends, it's hard to really know any of them well. If there's always a crowd milling around, how can you even hear yourself think, much less know what other people are thinking and feeling?

If this were a Shakespearian play, what you would do is tell everyone that you were going away on a long vacation, then you'd put on a disguise and come back to your friends as someone else. You would ask questions about yourself and set up little tests for these friends — "Are you going to take her favorite hair barrette, since she's not here to know about it?" Or you would say negative things about yourself and see if they defend you or not. Then, at the end of the play, you would reveal yourself, reward those people who were loyal to you, and send the others packing.

But since this is real life, and people generally get annoyed when you trick them and lie to them, let's try a different tactic.

The first thing I'd suggest is that you start hanging out with your friends in smaller groups, a few or even one at a time. Find out what these people really like to do and what they're really like. Discover whether you actually have anything in common. Did you have fun and feel great when you were around them, or did you (a) want to go home, (b) feel like you didn't belong there, or (c) feel like they didn't belong there? If it's any of these three, you probably weren't meant to be best friends with these people. You can still hang out in large groups, be nice to them, etc., but they fall more into the *acquaintance* category than the *friend* category. This is totally fine — not everyone is going to be a BFF or a bridesmaid in your wedding. There are billions of people in the world — chances are that everyone who looks for a friend is going to find one.

When you've found the people you have a good time hanging out with, who share your interests or personality traits, it's time to start "giving of yourself" to those people. That means make them cards on their birthdays (using plenty of glitter). Share your lunch. Stick up for them on the playground. If they seem upset, offer to listen. If they are happy about something, celebrate with them. And when you're giving of yourself, make sure to check out how a friend responds. If she seems pleasantly surprised, grateful, touched, and open to you, those are good signs.

If she seems hesitant, ungrateful, unsure what to do, or so enthusiastic about your generous nature that she starts trying to take advantage of you, uh, those are not good signs. It may be that person isn't connecting with you the way you thought. It may be that she has never had a real friend before and doesn't know how to respond when someone's really nice to her. It may be that she's the kind of person who expects others to do things for her all the time. Whatever. If someone isn't responding to your attempts at deeper, more genuine friendship in a positive way, it's time to rethink. That person might need to go onto the just-an-acquaintance list, or to the avoid-this-person-because-she-uses-people list.

Okay, so now you have a smaller group of people that you have a great time with and who you can trust to receive what you have to give. Time for the final test—what can they give when *you* need to receive? Try talking to these people about some of your problems (failing math, early onset of pimples, that kind of thing). Try asking them to help you celebrate when you've had something cool happen

"Okay, I guess I forgive you," Maggie said. "Only I don't see why you had to lie."

"Because I thought you were going to take Sophie away from me," Fiona said.

"Take her where?" Maggie said.

Fiona rolled her eyes at Sophie. "You know, become her best friend instead of me."

"Oh," Maggie said. "No, I never have best friends."

"There isn't any reason why we can't all be best friends," Sophie said as she crowded her mouth to the phone next to Fiona's. "You and me and Kitty."

Fiona looked like she suddenly had the stomach flu, but Sophie held up a wait-a-minute hand. "Fiona's my BEST best friend, but you and Kitty can be my other best friends and we can be yours and Kitty's."

Maggie didn't say anything for so long, Sophie wasn't sure she was still there. When she finally answered, she said, "Okay. I'll be over tomorrow."

When they hung up, Fiona was laughing. And laughing. And laughing.

"What?" Sophie said.

"I don't know," she said. "I just feel like laughing."

Sophie kind of did too.

(from *Sophie and the Scoundrels*)

(like passing math, getting rid of pimples). Or ask them to back you up when you need support (remember those bullies we talked about before?). Be careful—don't expect other people to totally take over the controls of your life or fix your problems. But loving support from friends is one of the great benefits of having them. If these people willingly share your joys and sorrows without trying to tell you who and how to be, they've passed the final test—these are your "real friends."

Is it okay to date a boy at twelve? What if you think he's a Christian?

Review the process we went through above about how to make sure that a friend is a real friend. Go ahead, I'll wait. Okay, that's a pretty intense process, right? I mean, that's going to take WEEKS, if not longer, and that's just with GIRLS—girls your age, girls who are at the same emotional and physical and social place that you are. I'm here to tell you, boys your age are none of these things.

Whether he's a Christian or not, the average twelve-year-old boy is completely and totally unprepared for the average twelve-year-old girl. Think about it. While you're busy relating to your friends and learning about your own style and trying to act more grown up and laughing one minute and crying the next, Joey Ravioli is still wearing the same jeans and T-shirt as ever, still wrestling around with the same big pile of guys he's been rolling in the dust with since he was three, still making that obnoxious noise with his armpit.

Girls are interested in guys, and they want those guys to feel for them the way they feel for the guys. They want emotional connection, like they have with their girlfriends. And what do guys want? For the most part, they don't even know, but it's definitely physical. That's why boys do things like take girls' stuff, bump into them on purpose, put ice down their backs, etc. They just want to touch them and get their attention. When they are with other guys, they do things like hit and push each other for fun, so why not with girls?

Anyway, what can dating possibly involve when you're twelve? If you both have parents who are okay with you two spending time together, they are going to have to be the ones to drive you places and pick you up—they'll always be around. Is that what you were envisioning? Probably not. I know just being able to say, "I'm dating Joey Ravioli," can make a person feel more mature, more adult, and very cool, but what does it really mean?

I think it's a good idea for girls and boys, around twelve years of age, to spend time together, especially in groups, doing things like playing sports, walking dogs, and being friends. It is possible to spend time with someone of the opposite sex and have a good time.

But why apply this extra layer of pressure? And why try to get ahead of the game? Dating is going to happen for you. Romance is in your future. Have fun looking forward to it, daydreaming about it, and becoming your true, totally, absolutely cool and irresistible self. When the time is right, Mr. Wonderful will detangle himself from the boy pile, change his clothes, brush up his vocabulary, and sweep you off your feet. When that happens, you want to be old enough and wise enough to still keep your head. That's a God-thing.

I haven't ever seen a fight at my school, but I hear about kids hurting other kids, like on buses, all the time on TV. And kids at my school will say, "I'm going to kick your butt!" or "I'm going to kill you!" Should I be scared about this? How do I keep from getting hurt?

There is actually less violence in schools today than there was when I was teaching high school. No, really. The reason for that is schools are a lot more vigilant about violence, a lot less tolerant of it, and they are finding ways to be more prepared for it. But television and other types of media know that people love a good story. When something like a bus beating or a school shooting happens in our country now, the story is all over everything we see — TV, magazines, newspapers, everything. That kind of coverage makes us feel like this kind of thing must be happening everywhere, *all the time*. Now, these are important issues, but how are you supposed to live your life when you're afraid to walk out of your house in the morning?

In the end, you can't control other people, but you can control YOU. You always have choices. First of all, go where you want to go and do what you want to do. Live your life, and don't walk around acting afraid. People who are looking for someone to pick on or hurt don't usually go for confident, assertive people — they go for people who look like they would be easy targets. Second, be aware of what's going on around you. Look, listen, and pay attention to the other kids on the bus or the playground or in the cafeteria. If you see trouble brewing, get yourself out of there and tell an adult who can help.

Third, when people say things like, "I'll get you!" or "I'll kill you!" usually they're just angry and blowing off steam, but those are threatening, powerful words. If it's someone you know, and you're involved in the situation, you can say to that person, "Hey, I know you're upset, but could you chill? It's not worth getting into a fight." If someone says something like that TO you, DEFINITELY say to them, "You know, I take that really seriously. Please calm down, or I'm going to go talk to the teacher (counselor, my mom, pastor, whoever is closest to hand)."

Our soccer coach had a son, and he died in a car accident. What should I say to my coach?

First of all, I am so sorry. It's horrible to lose a family member, especially a child. And one of the hardest things in the world is when someone you know is going through a painful time.

If you find yourself in this situation, it's important not to expect anything from the person when you approach him or her. Don't expect them to feel better, or be grateful, or even cry. People deal with loss and show grief in very different ways. So it's important to remember that this is one of those situations where it's not about you. This other person's need is so great and so real that you have to put your own discomfort aside. Now, it's not up to you to make it better, but it is up to you to offer what you can, as a friend, even though you're a young friend.

Honesty is always the best place to start. It's the all-occasion gift. If you see your coach, say, "I don't know what to say — I know I can't understand how horrible this is." Then offer what you can. Prayer is great — everyone can pray. Try, "I don't know what I can do to help, but I am praying for you. I just want you to know that I'm thinking about you." Knowing that someone else cares can help a person who is isolated in grief feel not so alone.

And go ahead and say what you feel. "I am so sad that your son died. I can't imagine how awful it is." It's okay to say what happened, and that it's horrible. It's not like it's a secret. This person knows his son died. He's probably not pretending it didn't happen, but sometimes the people around a grieving person do try to act like nothing occurred. They want to try and make things seem "normal" for them. That's usually not very helpful, but knowing that someone else is sad and knows what's going on can be.

If it's an adult who's grieving, like this soccer coach, you're

"I can do almost anything I want here in the hospital," Kitty said, "except be with you guys."

Her lower lip trembled, and Sophie could see what was coming.

"We brought you a basket, Kitty!" she said.

Maggie and Darbie hoisted the basket up beside Kitty, but she didn't even get a hand into it because the Corn Flakes pulled out each item and held it up to her and explained it—all at the same time. Kitty giggled through the whole thing and said thank you about a hundred times.

"Let's open them all!" Fiona said.

"Not right now," Kitty said. "I'm getting kinda tired." She sank against the pillows and sighed. Her eyelids drooped over her eyes.

The Corn Flakes stood on each side of the bed, looking at her.

"Should we go?" Sophie whispered.

"I have to have an operation."

They jumped as if Kitty had leaped off the bed.

"What kind of operation?" Maggie said.

Darbie nudged her. "You don't have to talk about it if you don't want, Kitty."

Kitty looked at all of the Corn Flakes. "I'm just scared," she said.

All the way home, Sophie held back something hard that was pushing against her chest from the inside, while everyone talked about everything but Kitty. As soon as she got her bedroom door closed and flung herself across the bed, Sophie's chest broke open and let the sobs and the tears come out.

It wasn't long before she felt her mother joining her on the bed.

"It's hard, isn't it, Dream Girl?" she said.

"You know what, Mama?" Sophie said into the bedspread.

"What?"

"There's nothing in that basket that's going to make Kitty better."

(from *Sophie's Stormy Summer*)

probably not going to be spending a lot of time with him or her. It's a little different if you have a peer who has lost someone, a friend your own age. You're more in a position to offer to let her talk, to listen, to put your arm around her and let her cry. There's still only so much you can do for someone who is grieving, but sometimes, even though we only have a little to give, it goes a long way. After time passes, you'll probably find out that honest, sensitive, heartfelt things did a lot for the person you offered them to.

What do you do when your friend gets grounded for a while and tells you she has no idea when she will be released? It's so boring to wait and wait. Plus it's even worse when your brother tells you your friend might be grounded till September! I mean come on, that's after school starts! And what if she's telling you she's grounded, but she's really not? How would I know?

First things first. Tell your brother to leave you alone and then ignore him. He doesn't know how long your friend is going to be grounded! What, did he have lunch with her mother? Did he and her father play golf together? He doesn't know, and he'll get bored with bothering you if he doesn't get a rise out of you.

Unfortunately, that's the only answer to this friend issue because there is no way to know how long your friend will be grounded. Maybe, if you don't know where to turn without her, it's time to think things through. Have a little "me time." Could you write in a journal, play with toys you haven't looked at in ages, listen to music and draw, watch your favorite movie? Could you take a walk around the yard, play with the cat or dog? And what about other friends? Is there someone you haven't spent time with in a while? Are there things you like to do but your grounded friend doesn't? Maybe you could do some of those things and not have to worry about her complaining or getting bored. See what you can come up with, because life is short, babe. Don't waste away pining for your imprisoned friend. It's not helping her, and it's definitely not helping you.

There is another huge issue in this question, and it's about trust. Remember trust, the precious, fragile gift two friends exchange?

We have two possibilities. One is that you are being totally paranoid — your friend shaved her father's head in the night, and consequently is grounded for seven months. She's telling you the truth. The other is that your "friend" is telling you that she's grounded in order to avoid spending time with you.

Let's say your friend WAS lying. You saw her with another girl from your class at the mall, and when you call and ask about it, there is a long, uncomfortable pause, and your friend either admits to lying or lies (obviously) some more, or just hangs up. Well then, as painful as it is, this particular individual is not, I'm afraid, your friend. She has broken trust. She's hurt you. If she doesn't want to spend time with you anymore, or you did something to upset her, she should have been honest about it. Tell your friend that she hurt you, and that you're angry. Then you should go cry and talk to someone you CAN trust, like your mom or another friend. Just be sure you're talking about how YOU feel, not gossiping about how horrible and terrible your friend is. That's not acceptable, no matter how mad you are.

Now let's revisit that paranoia thing, which is when you're absolutely convinced that someone is doing something, even though you have no evidence, or have evidence to the contrary. It happens to the best of us; sometimes it's hard trusting people who live in our very homes, much less people that we haven't seen for weeks and weeks. If there is no evidence your friend is lying, you can say to her, "I just need reassurance, because we haven't hung out in a long time—you are really grounded, right? You're not just avoiding me, are you?" A good friend may still say, "What are you talking about, weirdo?" but she'll do it with love, and she'll reassure you that it's all in your head.

"Solitary confinement makes you do weird stuff." Art leaned on the doorjamb. "So what have you being doing in here all weekend, writing a novel?"

Lily shrugged. She definitely wasn't going to tell him she'd been reading the Bible and then have him laugh at her. She'd have to throw something at him.

"I used to get grounded a lot when I was in middle school," Art said. "I was in my rebellious period. I grew out of it." Art gave half a grin. "Every time I got sent to my room for, like, fifty years, I'd get so bored that I'd clean it up. I think that's why Mom used that punishment so often. It was the only time you could see the floor."

Lily looked around at her neat bookshelves and the tidy top of her dresser. "Mine's always clean," she said.

"Yeah, well, you're little miss always-do-everything-right anyway."

"No, I'm not!" Lily said. "I hardly do anything right anymore!"

"You really oughta consider switching to decaf, Lil," he said. "You do more stuff right than anybody I know. You make me sick, you're so perfect."

(from *Lily and the Creep*)

You can also just leave well enough alone, and trust that your friend is telling the truth. It may be hard sometimes. It's going to take some work to control that little voice in your head that says, "No one REALLY likes you. They all want to get away from you!" That little voice is not a healthy instinct. It's actually you doubting yourself and your self-worth. You'll probably continue to have issues with it all of your life, but the more you tell that voice that you're not going to listen to it, the easier it gets.

chapter six

Sorry, You're Stuck with Them

Answers to Questions about Family

My sister thinks she is better than the whole world. She drives me crazy! How can I make her stop thinking she's so great all the time?

It's pretty common for sisters to drive us crazy. Very often they do crazy-making things, like "borrowing" our stuff without asking, blabbing all our embarrassing secrets, taking the last cookie, not sharing, getting more attention than us, and, in this case, thinking they're better than everyone else.

Whatever the case, it's pretty irritating when someone else is acting like they have more value than you do. Let's qualify that a little—it's *pretty* irritating when someone you barely know is acting like that. But it's *really* irritating when you live with someone who pulls that even a little bit of the time. Living in the same house as someone else is a whole different ballgame even than being BFF with somebody. All their faults, all their weaknesses—EVERYTHING they do that drives you nuts is magnified, like, a thousand times. This is because once you live in the same house with someone, there's this sense that you can't escape—you HAVE to live with it, and it's going to go on and on and on forever.

It took Sophie a minute to realize that Lacie's voice, and then Daddy's, were coming through the floor. Of course. This part of the attic was right above Lacie's room.

Sophie—Dr. Diggerty—tried to return to her work, but it was as if she were being pulled by the ear to listen to them.

"Yes, I hear Sophie talking to herself," Daddy said. "But I think that's going to stop soon. She's starting to change."

"Right," Lacie said.

"And I think it's because of you, Lace."

"Are you kidding? Daddy, she won't listen to a thing I say."

Sophie heard the chair creak, and she knew Daddy was sitting down on the corner of it.

"You might not think she's listening, but she's watching you," Daddy said. "That's one of the reasons I grounded her, so she'd be around you more often. You're a good role model for her."

"Thanks," Lacie said.

You have to be KIDDING! Sophie thought.

"You're always my go-to guy," Daddy said. "I know I can count on you."

As the chair creaked again and Lacie's door opened and closed, Sophie put her face into the pile of linens she'd pulled out of the trunk and decided this must be what it felt like to be an orphan.

(from *Sophie's Secret*)

But first, people do change and grow. And second, you are not going to live either with your parents or with your sister for the rest of your life. One of you will, most likely, move out sometime, and then it will be easier to keep from ripping out her nose hairs, one by one ...

But back to your question. How can you make her stop thinking she's so great all the time? Short answer? You can't. Sorry. We cannot *make* people do or not do things, especially not the things they do in their heads, like think. Not even your parents can change your sister's attitudes and beliefs. They probably have a lot of influence, because they've raised her and they provide for her and they have the power to punish her or reward her. There are things you could try to influence her behavior, some of them positive and some of them negative, but the solution to your problem is not in changing your sister.

There is, however, a way to solve the problem. You could try talking to your sister. Wait until she does something that you don't like. Then take a deep breath, and in a calm, controlled way (not in an angry, screaming, spit-flicking way), say something like, "You know, sis, when you do/say/act that way, it makes me think that you think you're better than I am. Is that what you think?" Then see what she says.

She may say, "Well of COURSE I'm better than you and most of the rest of America!" In that case, you're kind of back to square one as far as she goes. You could say to your sister, "Well, I'm sorry that you think that. I love you, but I don't think you're better than me or America, and when you act that way, it hurts my feelings. I don't want you to treat me like that anymore, and if you do, I'm telling Mom." She may or may not care. She might not have realized that she was hurting you, even if she does think she's better. Who knows? She might come around.

Or she may say, "What are you talking about? I don't think I'm better than you!" You gotta remember, she's a kid too, and just like you she's figuring out all this relating-to-other-people stuff. Hard as it is to believe (I mean, what is she, dense?) she might not realize that she's getting under your skin or bruising your feelings. It's really easy to take someone for granted, to not consider their feelings or wants, because you're so comfortable around them you almost forget that they're there. When someone is in your space almost all the time, it's like they're a part of you. So you start to naturally assume that if you're happy, that person's happy.

So I also suggest, after you've called your sister on her behavior in a nice, mature way, that you have some compassion for her — and yes, that you forgive her (are you seeing a pattern here?). Forgive her even if she keeps thinking and acting like she's better than the whole world. Don't let her put you down or walk on you. But remember that she's probably just in a phase, and you don't want to be mad at your sister. So let it go, and when all else fails, pray for patience. It sounds like you might need it.

> One of my blockages between me and God is not being able to control myself when my brother and sister annoy me. Most of the time, I admit, it is only a minor thing, but it really drives me crazy!!! I am trying to stop, but it is so difficult. It's like trying to keep a stray dog on a leash!! I was wondering if you could reply back to me with some helpful suggestions.

I'm impressed with this question for two reasons: One, the stray dog thing is a great metaphor, and two, you recognize that this problem isn't just with your brother and sister — it's with you and your relationship with God. Already tons of maturity here, obviously. Go, girl!

Like we were talking about before, when you live with someone who gets annoying, it's always much, much worse than an annoying classmate or acquaintance, because you basically can't get away from that person. And it is hard to stop how we feel about things. I think a lot of people fall into the trap of thinking that we have to

Sophie's six-year-old brother, Zeke, met her at the kitchen door when she got home. His face was smeared with jelly, and so was the doorknob, the front of the refrigerator, and the whole snack bar.

"Are you finger-painting with jam?" Sophie said.

Zeke scowled at her. Sophie grabbed his hand just before he dragged it across his sticking-up-all-over-the-place dark hair. He looked just like their father, minus the strawberry preserves.

"No," he said. "I was makin' me a sandwich."

"Where's Lacie?" Sophie said. "It's her day to play with you."

"She's not home yet," he said, "but I'm old enough to make my own snack."

"Yeah, but you're not old enough to paint the kitchen when you're done," Sophie said. "Does Mama know you're doing this?"

"No." Zeke climbed onto a stool at the snack bar where two pieces of bread were drowning in jelly. "I'm makin' her one too. It's a surprise."

"That's for sure," Sophie said.

(from *Sophie Loses the Lead*)

control how we feel, stop feelings in their tracks, and shut some kind of door on them. That actually isn't very healthy.

We have feelings for a reason. They are signals from our inner selves that help us know what to do. An emotion like irritation sends a very important message that you shouldn't ignore. It probably means a boundary has been crossed. Boundaries are imaginary lines that we ask people not to cross. There are certain ways that you don't want people to talk to you, touch you, or treat you, and if you tell people what your boundaries are, they are a lot less likely to trample all over them, either by mistake or on purpose.

I think Christians especially tend to get confused about boundaries. Jesus tells us to take care of our fellow human beings, to give unto others and focus on God instead of our worldly problems. But Jesus doesn't mean for us to let everyone walk all over us, or ONLY do things for other people and never ourselves. And he doesn't say that we should never feel bad about anything or never want anything. Now, Jesus was God on earth. Do you really think he would have said, "I know you were made with all these emotions and needs, and that you have lots of weaknesses, but I expect you to pretend your emotions don't exist and totally wear yourself out being everyone else's idea of perfect"? Uh, no. Jesus does not expect us to be perfect, and Jesus does NOT expect us to try and fulfill everyone else's needs while totally ignoring our own. God is the only one you don't need to have boundaries with.

So your brother and sister annoy you — they have crossed a line. Somehow, they are in your space. Maybe they're making noise, maybe they're actually touching you (don't you hate that?), maybe they took something of yours (what is it with little brothers and diaries?). Especially if they're doing it on purpose — probably to get your attention — it makes you want to lash out, yell at them, and chase them around the house with a stick. The more violent your reaction is, the more you've probably been storing up your feelings, trying to stuff them down and ignore them. The first time you stop stuffing your feelings and try to express them is going to be hard.

So you listen to your emotion, and when it says, "They're all over me! I need quiet! I need space!" the easiest thing to do is get up and get away from them. This isn't always possible, but if it is, try it. Don't look at it as being run off—see it as making a choice about what's best for your sanity, and seeking out the space you need.

Another thing to try is spelling it out for them. Tell them what your boundaries are, "Look, it's okay if you come in my room as long as you knock first. If you don't knock, you have to leave. And you can borrow my toys/clothes/books as long as you ask first and don't destroy them. If you don't ask or you break something, you can't borrow my stuff anymore. It's not okay, ever, for you to pull my hair, come bursting into the bathroom when I'm in the tub, or read my diary. I don't like it when you play rough or invade my privacy." Choose your battles when you're setting up boundaries, because you probably can't have absolutely everything the way you want it. It helps if you pick boundaries that your parents will back you up on.

You have to be consistent about boundaries once you've set them up. You can't totally be slack about your bro and sis trashing your stuff, then all of a sudden freak out on them. Every time something mysteriously disappears or breaks, you've got to say, "Where is my so-and-so? I don't remember saying anyone could use it. My stuff is now off limits until it comes back in one piece or someone tells me what happened to it." And you've got to involve your parents, so that you have authority behind your decree. Just so you're not leading anybody into temptation, put your stuff up high or in a closet if you have to. That's what locks are for.

If your siblings take the cue from you and start setting their own boundaries, you've got to respect theirs too. Don't borrow their stuff without asking, tickle them if they don't like it, or call them names that make them turn purple. By modeling respect, you'll be encouraging them to respect you. None of this is going to happen overnight, mind you. You and everyone else involved is going to backslide from time to time. But it will make your life a lot easier.

There is one more necessary authority to involve in all of this, and that's God. Instead of letting your annoyance with your brother and sister be a block between you and God, let it be a *bridge*. The stuff we're struggling the most with is the stuff we should go to God *with*. Besides, it's not like God doesn't know. So when you are feeling annoyed and about to go over the edge, turn to God and say, "God, I am SO ANNOYED WITH THEM! WHAT IS UP WITH THEM? WHY ARE THEY ABSURD LITTLE CREEPS WITH COOTIES?!!!" Let it all hang out.

Then review your plan with God. "Okay, I know you gave me these feelings so I can know what my boundaries are. I am going to calmly remove little Joey's hand from my hair and tell him he'd better find something else to do or I'm going to have to tell Mom that he's hurting me. I can also ask him what he really wants. If he needs me for something, there are better ways to get my attention — like just asking me for help."

Then ask for God's help, "God, please give me the strength and patience to follow through with my plan and not strangle Joey, because I don't want to be a strangler — I want to be a nice person."

Lately I've been really having a lot of emotional problems. I'm the second youngest of seven and almost all of my siblings have problems which adds to my problems: my sister is unmarried with three children, my brother has marital problems, my other brother lost his job, my eldest sister has problems with depression, and my little brother is just plain annoying. I am also struggling with suicidal thoughts, though I would never do anything. I've talked to my parents, but judging from your books, I think you probably understand how hard it is to talk to your parents about these things. Can you help me?

When I got this letter, I was VERY upset. When someone is having suicidal thoughts, which means they are thinking about killing themselves, it is serious business. I recommended that this young woman seek professional help for how she was feeling, and I really hope she did.

I hope, also, that she learned to stop taking on all the problems of her other family members. That's a really hard thing. We always want to help the people we love, especially our family members. When someone in the family has a problem, it's not uncommon for everyone else to put their lives on hold and help out. But that can only go on for so long, and while sisters and brothers can always be loving and supportive of each other no matter how old they are, it's never the job of a child, someone under the age of eighteen, to step in and help fix anyone else's problems. And it's really hard sometimes, especially with family, to know when we're just helping out and when we're acting like someone else's problem is our own.

If a member of your family is sad, you'll probably be sad for that person, but that doesn't mean you have to feel that way all the time too. If your brother has a problem that cancelled the family vacation or meant your mom couldn't drive you to basketball practice, it's okay to feel frustrated, disappointed, and even angry at the kid. You don't have to go stomping around and acting difficult — in fact, not stomping is one really great way to show love to a family member who is going through a hard time. Later you can say to your mom, "I know so-and-so needed our help, but I still feel upset that we couldn't go." It's never selfish or wrong to feel the way you feel or to try and talk about your feelings when they're starting to get kind of overwhelming.

The young woman who wrote me this letter describes problems of much older siblings at completely different stages in life than where she is, and she says that those problems are affecting her. Those things are completely out of her control and not her responsibility. She may feel sad for them and want to help, but all she can do is pray that their situations improve and offer them all the love and encouragement she has. She can give hugs, tell them she's thinking about them, and celebrate when something good does happen — and that is more than enough. It's never fair for children to suffer because of an adult's mistakes.

When you're the kind of person who wants to help others, the hardest thing in the world to learn is when to say, "That is not my problem." It feels like we're being cruel and not helping someone we love. But the times we learn the most and grow the most are when we figure out the answers ourselves, and that's true for everyone. So start now. Practice supporting friends and family with love and encouragement without taking on all the worry and effort of looking for the solutions for them. You will have a whole lot more to give, all your life long, if you put as much effort into your own happiness as you do into others'. It's a God thing.

My dad is sick (he has diabetes), so my grandma lives with us. I don't have a mom. I get really tired of my grandma telling me what to do, because it's completely different from what my dad tells me to do. If my dad dies, I have to stay with my grandma. What do I do?

I told you in the first chapter that my dad died of diabetes when I was fifteen, so of course, my heart immediately goes out to you. The first thing I noticed was how focused you are on the problems with your grandma and not on how sick your dad is. That's actually really normal. When something is as painful and scary and out of your control as death is, it's natural to focus on the problems you think you can do something about. So let's do that.

You have two authority figures in your life, and they're both telling you to do different things. That is confusing and frustrating in the best of situations, so when you're additionally faced with other big, scary problems, like your dad being really sick, it's got to make you want to start pulling all your hair out, one strand at a time. Each of these adults has a lot on his and her individual plate—one is sick, and the other is facing losing her son and the responsibility of raising her granddaughter. I have a lot of compassion for how hard it must be for each of them too.

But that doesn't mean they're not the adults anymore. That's the thing about being an adult: responsibility comes with it, no matter how old or sick you are. And even if you can't do something you used to be able to do, that responsibility doesn't go away. Your grandmother is already trying to tell you what to do because she knows she'll be taking over the responsibility for you. The trouble is, your father hasn't decided to stop taking care of that responsibility yet.

It's not your responsibility to fix this situation, of course. You shouldn't tell either of these adults how to be parents. But you do have a responsibility to yourself. You aren't getting what you need, which is consistency, and it is okay for you to sit down with your grandma and your dad and say, "Okay, you tell me to do one thing, and you tell me to do another, and I'm really confused and frustrated. Is there another way that we can do this? Can I at least know who I should be listening to?" Then you need to step back and let them work it out.

I imagine that the conflict you're feeling with your grandma is coming not only from being confused about who to listen to but also from the resentment you might be feeling about your grandma trying to take your dad's place. If your dad has always been the one to tell you what to do, it's going to be hard for you to adjust to someone else doing that. If your grandma and dad can come to some kind of agreement, then the transition you might have to make if your dad does pass away is going to be a lot easier for you.

Ages eight to twelve are a really, really hard stage in life. You are old enough to express yourself, old enough to take on some responsibility, but you're still a kid. You don't always know WHAT to express, and you don't always know HOW MUCH responsibility is really yours. And the people around you, even if they are older, aren't perfect, so some things they don't know either. What's cool is that, now that you're starting to want more control of your life, you can communicate your needs, start to participate in decisions about you, and earn others' respect. What's not cool is there's still so much control that you don't have. Yet sometimes you're going to be exposed to situations that are way bigger and scarier than fighting with your sister or getting your period — and those things can be pretty huge — it's good to know you'll still have help with the big things for a long time!

chapter seven

Certificate of Authenticity

Answers to Questions about Being Yourself

Why did you want to have the same name as Nancy Drew? Don't you want to be different from others and be your own person?

When I was younger, it wasn't so much about having the same name as Nancy Drew (and you have to admit, I was already halfway there) as it was about being like her. Yes, that does sound like I'm trying to be someone I'm not, doesn't it? Then again, sometimes we admire people because they possess good qualities and inspire us to try and develop those qualities in ourselves. That leads us to changing in positive ways, and it's not the same thing as trying to be exactly like someone else.

If I didn't think it was okay to try to emulate—which is not the same as imitate—people you think are really great, I wouldn't spend so much time trying to be a role model. When you emulate someone, you don't try to be them exactly—you try and apply the things you admire about them to yourself and your life in your own way. Someone I admire is Maya Angelou. I don't try to imitate Maya Angelou—I don't wear African prints or write books of

During after-lunch free time that day, Sophie and Fiona were near the monkey bars. Sophie crouched on the ground beside Fiona, holding her hand and stroking her forehead.

"Now what are y'all doing?"

Sophie tried to ignore the sound of Julia's voice. Henriette had scarlet fever—this was no time for conversation.

"Hello? Anybody home?"

Sophie finally looked up at her least favorite faces on the playground.

"We're playing a game," Fiona said.

"I know that," Julia said.

Fiona blinked her gray eyes. "Then why did you ask?"

"Well," Julia said, "because you're lying on the ground and Soapy is patting your head like you're a cocker spaniel."

"You should get up off the ground, Fiona," a skinny girl said. Her voice was thick, as if she still had some kind of nose problem.

"Tell me why, Anne-Stuart," Fiona said to the skinny girl. "Is there a rule against lying down outside?"

"There ought to be," Julia said. "There ought to be a rule against being weird, period."

"But who says what's weird and what's not?" Fiona said.

(from *Sophie's World*)

poetry. But I do weawr clothes that express who I am, and I do try to stand up for what I believe and express what I believe through my writing. Just because someone inspired me to do those things or because other people do those things too, doesn't mean I'm not being different or my own person.

Being your own person isn't always about being different — it's about making choices based on who you really are inside, whether those choices are what to wear, what music to listen to, or how you should handle a difficult situation. We all try to imitate sometimes. We have to if we want to learn to walk, talk, write, or be a part of any group of people. It's part of how we learn. But eventually, you get to the point where you have the skills you need. Then you can apply them however YOU want, not necessarily the same way someone else does. When you get there, you have to look inside yourself and find out who God created you to be. And then you start draggin' her out in the open.

I have a big problem. I always think I'm a geek and different. I can't believe people would even want to hang out with me! I have a lot of embarrassing, stupid moments — I feel I have the most stupid moments in the world! I have prayed and prayed to God about my problem. I have also talked to my mom about it and she is no help. Can you please give me advice?

You may actually be a geek. You probably are different, and I can guarantee you have stupid moments, because everyone in the universe has plenty of stupid moments. Your problem is that when you view these facts, you think about them in a negative way.

What is a geek? Someone who loves Star Trek? Someone who gets good grades? Someone who has long legs and arms and is clumsy? I had to look it up online, because my dictionary was published in 1957, and I found out the first recorded use of the word *geek* was in 1876, and it meant "fool." It soon came to mean "a carnival performer whose act consists of bizarre or morbid feats, such as biting the heads off chickens." Somehow this word transformed from "chicken-head-biter-off-er" to "someone with technological expertise but who is often socially inept or offensive."

So unless you have troubles prying yourself away from your computer screen, you're not a geek. But if you are, so what? Who gets to say it's bad if computers are your thing? What's happening here is that you are allowing other people's expectations to influence your view of yourself. When it comes to our likes, our dislikes, and our self-expression, that's just not up to other people.

It's the same thing with thinking that being different is bad. *Different* just means "not alike" or "unusual." Why are these things negative? I've spent, and will continue to spend, a lot of my time trying to change that view, because different can be really good, especially when it's an authentic difference and not difference for the sake of being unlike everybody else. Everyone is different, in some way, from everyone else. God made us that way. If God made us different, can it really be bad?

You've got to be you, even if it means sometimes acting stupid and feeling embarrassed. *Stupid*, as we know, is "slowness, lacking mental ability," and sometimes that's all of us. No one always has the right answers every second of the day and night. So, if you have a moment when you weren't thinking as quickly or clearly as you usually do—unless that moment made you do something really wrong—you don't need to get all red-faced about it. And look at it this way, "stupid" moments make the best stories.

You're not going to be perfect and on your game one hundred percent of the time — you're just not. If you expect to be perfect, you're going to exhaust yourself. And if you can't see the humor in your own mental lapses, you're going to be miserable for the rest of your life.

But you should still be open to helpful suggestions or criticism that come from people who care about you and want to help you improve in some way, especially when you love and trust them. But being perfect or the same or unembarrassed or un-geek-like is not required to live a very cool life.

How am I supposed to be authentic?

Way to get right to the heart of it, girlfriend! Okay, let's do this!

Step One: In order to tell whether or not you are being authentic, you have to have a kind of standard of authenticity to measure against. Like the official YOU yardstick. The YOUSTICK.

You don't have to create the youstick — it already exists — but you do have to find it. Uncover it. It's in you, in your heart and your head, underneath all the stuff people keep telling you to do and be all the time. Everyone has a youstick, but they're not all the same, obviously, or we would all be alike. Still, they all have similar dimensions — four sides, in fact. Each youstick has an honesty side, a health side, a justice side, and a love side. And each youstick operates based on your feelings. When you use it by comparing something to it, it tells you whether or not that thing is YOU by sending you an emotional reaction. That gives you your answer.

Step Two: Start comparing things to the youstick. Start with little, not-as-important things: That bracelet you HAD to have because everybody else was wearing one. Being a cheerleader like your best friend. Owning every CD your older—and very cool—cousin has.

Take things one by one and hold them up to the youstick. Do that by asking the four youstick questions about honesty, health, justice, and love.

- "Is this honestly what I like/how I feel? Does this honestly express me?"
- "Is this healthy for me—does it make me feel good physically, emotionally, and mentally?"
- "Is this fair to me and other people? Am I taking something away from others or myself by doing this?"
- "If I do this am I showing love for myself and others?"

Even if you have a hard time getting yes or no answers to these questions, you will get a feeling, maybe in the pit of your stomach, maybe in your chest.

Step Three: It's now up to you to figure out what the feeling the youstick sent you means. Here's a helpful feelings chart that may help:

Physical Sensation	Emotion	You or Not You?
Heaviness in your stomach	Guilt, Dread	Not you
Tightness in your chest	Anxiety, Fear, Sadness	Not you
Relaxing of your whole body, a feeling of lightness	Happiness, Relief	You

Tension throughout your whole body, clenching of hands, feet, teeth, or any individual muscle	Irritation, Anger, Anxiety	Not you
Shaky, jumpy, can't sit still	Anxiety, Fear, Uncertainty	Not you
Fast breathing, heart racing, wanting to run away and hide	Fear	Not you
Raised voice, tense body, can't sit still, desire to yell, throw or hit something	Anger	Not you
Tears, choking sensation in your throat, whole body feels heavy, burning eyes	Sadness	Not you
Relaxed body, clear head, even breathing, regular heart rate	Peacefulness, Certainty	You

Step Four: After using the chart to correctly identify your emotion and whether or not something is YOU or not, act accordingly. If it is you, go for it, and if it isn't you, don't ... WITH the following exceptions.

Let's say something REALLY feels like you, like dying your hair purple. Your parents may still put the kibosh on that, and you should listen to them and not go behind their backs and dye your hair. First, it's really hard to express yourself when you're grounded, and second, sometimes being YOU isn't easy. Maybe you were meant to have purple hair, but that doesn't mean everyone's going to accept that. Your school may have rules about that kind of thing. Or maybe you're a really sensitive person, and your parents know people are going to tease you and you're going to want to curl up in a ball for three weeks. In this case, they aren't trying to keep you from being you so much as protecting other parts of you. When you are older, and less susceptible to teasing, and in a situation where rules and regulations like that don't apply, break out the rubber gloves and the dye bottle, if that's what you still want.

And let's say something REALLY doesn't feel like you, like going to bed at nine p.m. and getting up at seven a.m. Some people do have internal sleep patterns that make them want to sleep during the day and be up at night. But those people still probably have to attend the fifth grade, which starts at 8:30 a.m. and requires the fuel of at least eight hours of sleep to function. This is another case of this-is-the-way-it-goes-right-now—sometimes we can't control our environments. The school and your parents aren't trying to deny who you are. They have to function within guidelines too, and want you to have the right amount of sleep and legally required education. When you are older and still want to sleep during the day and do stuff all night, you can get a job as a midnight disc jockey or security guard or nurse or lab technician—or one of those people who analyzes people's sleep patterns!

But some things are never okay to compromise, even if an adult tells you otherwise—like your boundaries about your body, being treated with love and respect (and treating other people that way), and your relationship with God. On the big issues, it is okay to put up a fuss, even with an adult. Of course, to find out the best WAY to put up a fuss, you should check with the youstick.

Step Five: Repeat as often as necessary. Don't be afraid to share your knowledge about the youstick with others. Just remember that each youstick is personalized, handcrafted by the Master Youstick Maker for each individual. One person's youstick cannot always be used successfully by or for another person.

I like to think that this generation of young women is freer to be themselves than past generations have been. You can play sports (and that wasn't always possible, even for girls MY age), plan to be anything you want (even when I was a kid it was unusual for a girl to want to be a doctor or a truck driver), and stand up and speak out for the things you believe in (which was still considered pretty un-girl-like when I was a tween). I LOVE that! You have SO many chances to develop the courage and the wisdom it takes to be who you are, and I hope you will take those chances just the way God wants you to—even though you're faced with WAY tougher things than I was at your age.

Lily holed up in her room with her Talking to God journal and her dog Otto. He busied himself chewing on an old toothbrush he'd pulled out of the trashcan while Lily poured out her dilemma to God.

I think it was a miracle that I got elected, she wrote, *which means you meant for it to be. Please work on Mom and Dad so they'll see that.*

And please let me get along with that Ian kid, even though he's a boy. And please don't let Kresha and Reni feel left out. And please make me the best president of the seventh grade that ever was.

Lily paused to consider that last request. From what Art had said, it wasn't going to be that hard to surpass everybody else who had ever held the office.

But I'm still going to be amazing, God, she wrote. *I just have to be positive.*

(from *Lily Rules*)

chapter eight

What It's All About

Questions about Faith from the Tween Trenches

Do you have any tips for how to strengthen my faith and better my walk with God and things like that?

Do I!

Strong faith and walking with God come from two things—hearing God within you and seeing God when you look around you. When you feel like God is with you, inside and out—even in the bad times—then you know that you really are building your faith muscles and walking your God path.

It takes a lot of hard work to get to the point where you feel like God is around all the time. We can know that God is everywhere through what we hear at church and what we read in the Bible, but humans are funny that way. We know something in our heads, but until we've experienced it, felt it, been surprised by it, and tested it, we don't *know* it. And even after we *know* something, sometimes we can use a little review. Over the years, I've come across some tools that really help.

The first tools are for looking inside myself. I try to do two things every single day — write in a journal and study the Bible. I usually do this in the morning, because I'm one of those people who wakes up ready to do the day, and I also have the kind of life where I get to decide what happens when. (Nice, huh?) It might work better for you to do these things after school or before you go to bed.

I write three pages every day in my journal. I write about whatever comes into my head, even if I can't think of anything. Then I write, "I can't think of anything to write." Journaling helps me sort out what's going on inside me, how I really feel about it, and what I really want to do. Remember the youstick I talked about in chapter seven? This is like quality time with the youstick. Sometimes it helps to get it down on a piece of paper so you can look at it.

This kind of writing isn't at ALL like what you do in school. Get this: handwriting doesn't matter, spelling doesn't matter, whether it's interesting doesn't matter. This isn't your first novel! As a writer, that was hard for me at first, because I used to want everything I wrote to be this polished piece of literature. This brings me to the only really important rule about journaling: NOBODY gets to read your journal. If you're really going to be able to put down all your honest thoughts and feelings, you can't be worried about what other people are going to think when they see it. It's got to be totally private. Journaling helps you clear your head so you can work with some of the outside tools I'm going to talk about in a minute.

The other inside tool is studying the Bible. The Bible is basically a how-to guide for having faith and walking with God, but sometimes it's like the directions that come with something that was made in another country: "Open the hole device and into this you put. Shimmy well!" What? In order to follow directions like that, you have to pick up whatever it is and look at it from all angles and try to figure out how the directions translate into the real world. The Bible was written in another country (several, in fact), in several different languages (most of which no one speaks anymore, with a few exceptions), and thousands of years ago. It has been translated so many times we've lost count. It can be confusing.

So what you've got to do is take the confusing directions—the Bible—a little bit at a time each day. Read them, and then compare them to the thing they were written for—you and your life—and say, "What do these words mean to me, about me, for me?" A really helpful way to riddle it out and keep track of what you've learned is—shock and surprise—journaling! This is a separate journal from your totally private one. You can share this one if you want to, but just be careful, it's still personal. The entries can be as short or long as you need them to be. You just jot down what passage you read, what your thoughts are, and how you think it applies to you. If you don't know, keep thinking about it. It will come to you. Really look around in your life. Ask other Christians what they think.

I've read the whole Bible this way lots of times. I don't go from start to finish. I use what's called the lectionary, which is the schedule by which some churches read the Bible so they get through the whole thing in a certain period of time. There are lots of guides out there that can help you read the Bible in a year, or you can just take as long as you need to, reading however much you want to in a day.

Once you've started work on the inside, you have to turn and look outside yourself, because your relationship with God doesn't just show up in all that one-on-one time. It also appears in your relationships with others. Remember the whole wherever-two-or-more-are-gathered-in-my-name thing? Yeah, that counts even when you don't like that other person. You strengthen your faith and your walk with God through the choices you make when you're with others.

There are a couple of words Jesus uses a LOT—love and mercy—and one thing he tells pretty much everyone to do—pray. So these are good places to start. When you interact with oth-

Dr. Peter told them all to settle back in their bean-bags and close their eyes.

"I'm going to read Matthew twelve, verses one through eight," he said. "So get ready to imagine."

Sophie never had to do much getting ready. She loved this way of studying the Bible.

"Jesus has been teaching for a while now," Dr. Peter said. "People are starting to believe what he's telling them, and that doesn't make the Pharisees happy."

I hope we don't have to imagine we're one of them, Sophie thought. The Pharisees were the ones who were always trying to make everybody follow a bunch of strict rules and bad-mouthing Jesus.

"Pretend in your mind that you are one of the disciples," Dr. Peter said.

Sophie grinned to herself. *Now you're talkin',* she thought.

"'At that time Jesus went through the grain fields on the Sabbath,'" Dr. Peter read. "'His disciples were hungry and began to pick some heads of grain and eat them.'"

Although Sophie would rather have dreamed up a hot order of fries, she tried to imagine herself plucking the top off a stalk of wheat and munching away as she hurried to get up closer to Jesus. She didn't want to miss a word he said.

(from *Sophie Flakes Out*)

ers, think about others, and talk to others, try to make sure you're doing it with love. Love takes many forms, and the easiest one to use with everyone is respect. This is when you make the effort to understand what other people are thinking and see their side of things. You're less likely to be a jerk to people, even if they are really, really nasty to you.

Get into the habit of praying whenever you can. Not necessarily out loud or with other people, although that's okay too. A prayer can be in your head, quickly, when you have a second — like an Instant Message to God, or like a phone call, or sometimes like a really long, handwritten letter in your best handwriting. It depends on the situation. Sometimes prayer involves venting; sometimes it's asking a question; sometimes it's a big old shout of, "Hey! THANKS!" You're just keeping in touch as often as you can. You may not, at first, think you hear back. But the more you go inside and outside and practice finding God there, the more you WILL hear back.

You'll write things in your journals you didn't know you knew but make a lot of sense. You'll understand other people in ways you didn't think you were capable of. And things will start to seem like they're working out for the best somehow, even if it's not what you thought you wanted. You just have to keep at it. The more effort you put in, the easier it will get.

Well, sort of. It's not like life is going to be perfect. It's not like you're going to walk around every second thinking *I see God there and there and there and there.* You are always going to have to carve time out of your day and work around people who want you to do dishes and answer the phone and make dinner and do your homework and walk the dog. You are always going to have to struggle with yourself to treat others with love and mercy when they cut you off in the lunch line, take credit for your group project even when they didn't DO anything, talk behind your back, and take the last doughnut. It is going to be hard to remember to pray when you have a great day or when the TV is on all evening or when you have fifty math problems to do or when you're so tired at night you just want to get in bed without even brushing your teeth or changing into pajamas. Like I said, it's work.

And let's not forget about that amazing Jesus-thing called *grace*. You can work hard and be wonderful. But what really makes all that possible is God working in you, giving you the kind of faith Jesus showed us, letting his Holy Spirit guide you. Isn't it just the best to know you can't manage it all yourself? When you live your life as a God-thing, the big word is, well, God!

I went to Russia last year where there is a lot of poverty. I was very sad to see people standing on the sidewalks holding up bowls for money.
I feel now that I should be a missionary. There is a lady I know who goes to Russia at Christmas to help with orphans, but I need advice.
Should I be with my family or help in Russia?
I think God wants me to do missions.

What I love about your generation is that you're more aware of problems in the world than my generation was at your age, and you are convinced you need to go out there and do something about it. You want to find solutions, and that's a very powerful thing. You've experienced what is known as a "call." That's when a person feels like she has discovered her purpose, and she feels so strongly about it, she is willing to give up things we wouldn't dream of going without — like Christmas with our families, for instance.

Being a missionary is a pretty big deal. It's really hard work. It can be very frustrating and dangerous, and it can be really, really lonely. In spite of all the hard stuff, the people who answer the call love it. If you think you feel the call to be a missionary, I am not going to tell you to deny it. But I'm also not going to tell you to catch the next plane to Russia.

Before you run off to dedicate yourself to something as big a deal as being a missionary, you need to make sure you have completed some of the other, mini-missions you were put here to accomplish, like, I don't know, learning long division? Figuring out how NOT to hang your little sister by her thumbs? Discovering how to pray?

There are some things you can do on the path to help realize your dream of being a missionary. There are mission trips like the ones I used to go on with Susie Shellenberger from *Brio* magazine. She still takes hundreds of girls to places like Bolivia and Costa Rica and Brazil to do mission work and tell people about the love of Jesus Christ. There are missions right here in the United States (remember, we have poor, lost, troubled people too) that you can help out in your spare time. Your church may even have one. And you can start your own mini-mission — raise money for something, make things to give to people, or start a prayer campaign.

I don't think of myself as a missionary, but what I do as a writer is like my mission — it's my call. So if you're not a person who feels called to Russia or Bolivia or India, just listen for what your call is (and that may take you well into your adult life). Like Paul says in those New Testament letters like Romans and Ephesians, we all have different gifts. If you are a missionary at heart, try to keep this one last thing in mind: we don't have to give up every single last thing we have in order to be good Christians. We give what God inspires and requires us to, and in order to do that we have to have things like food, sleep, and spiritual fulfillment too. Taking care of yourself, especially now at a young age, helps ensure that you'll be able to take care of others, now and later, here or far away.

My parents think I have "spiritual problems" and that I don't really know God well at all. That's not true. I just have a more private relationship with God, and I don't always shout it out to people the way my "spiritually developed" sister does. They think that I don't read the Bible or pray, but I do, just in my own way! Is it bad to do it like that? What should I do if my parents think I'm not doing very well with God? They're kind of hard to talk to about spiritual things.

It is NEVER bad to read the Bible or pray in ANY way. If you are trying to have a relationship with God, and doing it in the way that works best for you, you are doing a GREAT thing. Not everyone is the same, not even if they are as closely related as parents and kids.

Your mom and dad have a lot of wisdom and experience. And they love you and want what's best for you. They can provide examples, put you in positive environments, and set boundaries for you. But when it comes to something as per sonal as your relationship with God, they can't tell you what's right for you. You and God have to figure that out.

I would encourage any young person who has a problem like this to go to his or her parents and say, "I want to talk to you about my relationship with God." It's going to be difficult because you'll have to get them to listen and make yourself vulnerable by talking about your personal relationship with God. Set an appointment with them—a time when it's just you and them. Make it a time when everyone expects to sit down and talk, with no TV and no interruptions, a time when no one is tired or emotional or distracted (the way they are when they've just come home from work). Then you can explain how you pray, how you read the Bible, and why that works for you.

All of this might be easier if you had the kind of ally—like a youth pastor, minister, or Sunday school teacher—who could add a little authority and maturity to your side. Is there someone who would be willing to sit down with you and your parents? Someone who understands that there are lots of ways to relate to and learn from God in the Christian faith?

The other thing you might do is go to the Bible. Use examples from the Bible to explain yourself. This will give your parents comfort that you are relying on God. There's a lot of material in the Bible about people having different relationships with God. Check out the prophets. They all had different ways of relating to God. Then there's Jesus. He called different people to do different things. The belief in the saving love of Jesus is the same, but the ways of relating are different because the needs are different. Have you read the book in the Lily series called *The Uniquely Me Book*? It goes into a lot of detail about different spiritual gifts, and even has some fun quizzes for you to take to find YOUR gifts.

The one thing your parents may be concerned about is whether you are sharing your faith. Jesus said we don't light a lamp to hide it under a bushel—he didn't give us faith so we could keep it all to ourselves. Make sure that all the things you're learning about the Lord in your quiet time are shining out in your life somehow. That's what makes God smile—and hopefully your parents too!

Every time I sit and try to talk to God, it seems that I am bombarded with a million different voices telling me things I need to do. Every time I try to sit still and read my Bible or just love God, I can't focus— sometimes I even get afraid, because the quiet just gets unbearable. Can you tell me what to do in quiet times so I can be with God?

While we all need to talk to God and read the Bible, there's nothing that says we have to be absolutely silent to do it. Start by talking to God, loving God, and being with God when you are in motion. You could listen to loud Christian rock music, giving praise or asking questions while you're taking a walk or a jog. You could serve others with physical activity—walks to raise money for treating diseases or for missionaries, playing with younger kids who are in the hospital or an after-school program, or cleaning the church. Get creative. How can you bring God into the crazy, fast-paced, always-moving life that you live?

It is helpful to be quiet and still sometimes. Even if it's in your nature to be running all around twenty hours out of every day, it still might be easier to get messages *from* God if you stop to take a breather. You can't expect yourself to be able to just DO this automatically if you're not used to silence or if it freaks you out. You've got to work up to it. It's just like you couldn't run a marathon tomorrow without training. Start by setting aside thirty seconds of stillness once a day. Go to a quiet place—no TV or siblings or your computer telling you that you have mail. Set an actual timer and put it where you can hear it but not see it. You can close

---

"At home," Dr. Peter said, "I want you to picture Jesus. And then I want you to talk to him about all these problems you're having."

"You mean, out loud?" Sophie said.

"It doesn't have to be out loud. You can whisper, or you can just think it in your mind. Just be perfectly honest with him. You don't have to worry about what he thinks, because he already loves you totally. Just talk to him every day, even just for a few minutes."

"Am I supposed to imagine him answering me?" Sophie said.

Dr. Peter shook his head. "No. That's where it's different from your other daydreaming. You'll need to let him talk for himself."

Sophie could feel her eyes popping. "He's going to answer me? Like, out loud?"

"Probably not out loud like your father's voice or mine. Some people hear the Lord that way, but I personally don't."

"Then how?" Sophie said.

"I can't tell you exactly. You might feel something peaceful. Or you might not feel anything right away, but then later you'll realize something has changed." He smiled. "Sometimes Jesus gives silent answers."

(from *Sophie's World*)

---

your eyes, or not. Take deep, slow breaths until the timer goes off. Focus on your body at first, on just keeping it still and breathing in and out. Let your mind do whatever it wants. Do this every day until thirty seconds seems like a piece of cake. When that happens, try sitting still and breathing in and out for one minute. After that gets easy, start adding minutes one at a time.

When you get to the point where you can sit still for five minutes, it's time to start focusing on your mind. Set your timer for five minutes, put it aside, and then pay attention to what comes into your head. Don't judge what you are thinking or try not to think or scold yourself for thinking too many things. Just pay attention to your thoughts as if they were a litter of puppies all trying to get your attention. Pet each one of them, one by one, starting with the yippiest, jumpingest one.

When you are comfortable with five minutes, try this: Each time a thought comes up, pray about it really quickly. Just think, "God, I need help with this," or "God, I'm really grateful for this," or "God, please remember that friend—she's sad." If you get distracted and lose track, it's okay. Pick right up again with the next thought that comes and concentrate on that.

You may find that as you pay a little attention to each thought not so many things pop into your head anymore.

If you really do feel activated all the time and can't ever focus on more than one thing for a few seconds, especially in school or when you're doing your homework, you should talk to your parents about maybe seeing a doctor. A doctor may be able to offer some simple and helpful suggestions.

God is in the quiet moments and the noisy moments too. You can find God anywhere you look, because God is always with you. It's good to have more than one way of relating, to be flexible, even though we'll always have our own favorite ways, different for each of us. You don't have to force yourself to be something you're not, but by trying something new, you could learn a lot about yourself that you didn't know yet.

I live in a kind of scary neighborhood, and a lot of people here drink and do drugs. My mom and sisters and brothers and I go to church almost every week, and most of my neighbors do too. The people there, like our youth minister, talk about God's love and God's kingdom, but sometimes I think that just can't be real. How can God let all this horrible stuff happen?

Part of the reason I write the books and teach the workshops that I do is to try and reach out to girls like you who don't have all the safety and security and happiness that all kids should. I want my readers to feel like there is something out there for them, something better, and someone who understands how hard it can be for them.

So this is what I think. God gave all of us what we call "free will." That's the ability to make our own choices. We get to decide whether to do the right or the wrong thing. Sometimes people make bad choices, and sometimes bad things happen. They don't always do it on purpose, but that doesn't make it any better.

But free will isn't all bad, because we also have the ability to make good choices—choices that help, and show love, and change things for the better. This is where God's kingdom comes in. I like to think that God's kingdom is where everyone is making good choices all of the time because they are all so much their God-selves that they always know what the right thing to do is, and they choose to do it.

And I also think this is where God's love comes in. God loving us isn't about God making everything perfect for us. God loves us no matter what we do to ourselves or others, so we don't have to be so ashamed of mistakes that we make or try to hide from God. Some people have made terrible, terrible mistakes, but God loves those people just as much as God loves us — unconditionally. So everyone always has the chance to make a good choice, even after making a bad choice. Everyone has a chance to join the kingdom. That's the love part.

It doesn't take away or fix how terrible things can be sometimes. What it does, is give us the power to love and change the world for the better no matter who we are and where we come from. And God will help you do that. That's the only way it's going to happen. That's what I want for all my readers. In fact, that's what I want for everyone.

P.S.
Signed, Sealed, Delivered

When we decided to do this book, we thought, "This will be so cute and fun!" It has been fun, and I sure hope you think the design is cute—I do! But it turned out to be a lot ... deeper than we were expecting it to be. I probably shouldn't be surprised, because I don't write cutesy, fluffy books for you, my precious readers. I try to write about real problems and situations girls face—so it follows that girls would ask me real questions, not cutesy, fluffy ones.

This became a book about being as real to my readers as they have been with me over the years, trying to show that the way I write my books is the way I try to live my life. It became about inspiring girls to be who and what they are, to be brave and creative and honest, not through characters or stories, but just flat out by saying it. Writing all these answers felt like sitting face-to-face with every one of you. It was fun and hard and sad and exciting.

I want to know more about what you're experiencing and wondering about, so keep your questions coming. Drop me a line! Send emails, send postcards, send homing pigeons. And never stop asking questions.

Never be afraid to get out there and find out what you need to know to be the best YOU that you can be. I'll be here. I'll be waiting to hear from you.

Love,
Nancy

Nancy Rue
PO Box 217
Lebanon, TN 37088
nnrue@hughes.net
www.nancyrue.com

1

Lucy wrote, "Reasons Why I Hate Aunt Karen," then she stopped and rolled the pen up and down between her palms. Dad always said "hate" wasn't a people-verb. It was a thing-verb. It was okay to hate jalapeno peppers in your scrambled eggs, which she did, and rock music that sounded like soda cans tumbling in a clothes dryer, which Dad did. It wasn't okay to hate human beings. Even Osama bin Laden. Or Aunt Karen.

Lucy drew a squiggly line through her words and wrote below them,

Reasons Why I Wish Aunt Karen Would Move to Australia:

Dad would say that was fine. Not that she was going to read it to him. Or anybody else. This was extreme-private stuff.

Lucy scowled at the page. The scribble messed it up, and she wanted to be so careful writing in this book. Anything to do with Aunt Karen made her mess up worse than usual. She would have to put that on the list of reasons. But she started with,

— Because Australia is as far away from me and Dad and Los Suenos, New Mexico, as she can get.

— Because she probably wishes our cats would move there.

The very round, coal-colored kitty on Lucy's pillow raised her head and oozed out a fat meow.

"Don't worry, Lollipop," Lucy said. "You're not going anywhere."

The cat gave Lucy a long, doubtful look before she winked her eyes shut, but she continued her nap with her head still up, as if she wanted to be ready to leap into the blue-and-yellow toy chest that Lucy kept propped open with a wooden spoon—for just such occasions—should the cat carrier, or Aunt Karen, appear.

Lucy leaned against her giant stuffed soccer ball, propped her feet on the blue-tile windowsill above Lollipop, and went back to the list of reasons.

— Because she wants me to learn to give myself a manicure.

She looked down at her gnawed-to-the-quick fingernails and snorted out loud.

— Because she says a ponytail isn't a real hairstyle.

Lucy flipped hers so it play-slapped at the sides of her face. She could see its blondeness out of the corners of her eyes. Yellow and thick and straight like her mom's had been. Not all weird and chopped-off and sticking out the way Aunt Karen's did. That was supposed to be a "style."

Lollipop's legs startled straight, and her claws sunk into Lucy's faded blue-and-yellow plaid pillowcase. She sprang to the windowsill—in the slow-motion way her chunky body insisted on—and pressed whisker-close to the glass. Lucy crawled to the headboard and leaned on it to peer out.

Granada Street was Saturday-afternoon-in-January quiet. Even J.J.'s house across the road looked as if it were trying to nap behind the stacks of firewood and tangle of rusted lawn mowers and pieces of cars piled around it. Dad asked Lucy just the other day if the Clucks still had everything but the kitchen sink in their yard. She reported that now there actually *was* a kitchen sink out there.

But there were no doors banging or Cluck family members yelling, which was what usually made Lollipop switch her tail like she was doing now. Unless the kitty saw something in the spider shadows of the cottonwood trees on the road, there was nothing going on out there.

At least it wasn't Aunt Karen already.

Lucy sank back onto the bed on her stomach, legs in a thoughtful kick. She pulled the top of her sweatshirt over her nose and mouth and wrote,

— Because she says clean jeans and a shirt with no writing on it don't count as Sunday clothes.

Aunt Karen said on the phone she was bringing Christmas presents.

"It won't be soccer cleats or a new seat for my dirt bike, I can guarantee you that," Lucy said to Lollipop. "You wait—it'll be some flowered dress." Whatever it was, it would make her feel like she was wearing sandpaper.

Lollipop rolled off the sill and burrowed herself between Lucy's pillows. Lucy didn't blame her. Aunt Karen hadn't even arrived yet and she was ready to hide under the pillows too. She set the book carefully on the bedspread and grabbed her soccer ball—the real one—between her feet and stretched her denim-clad legs in the air.

What was wrong with jeans and sweatshirts and tennis shoes in winter, and shorts and T-shirts and bare feet in summer? Nobody but Aunt Karen seemed to care what Lucy wore, but she couldn't come from El Paso without bringing skirts and bracelets and hair bows.

Lucy lowered the ball to the pillow beside Lollipop, sat straight up, and wrote one more thing—

— I wish Aunt Karen would move to Australia because she is nothing like my mother. Nothing.

She let the book sigh shut and smoothed her hands over its cover. Pale green with gold leaves she could feel under her fingertips. And gold letters too, which said, A WOMAN'S BOOK OF LISTS—not curly and girly, but clear and strong.

Lucy pulled the book to her nose and breathed in. In spite of how long it must have been in the box in the storage shed, it still smelled like Kit Kat bars and lavender soap, and it made Lucy sure her mom could be right outside her door, wanting to know if Lucy was finished with the book for now because she wanted to write in it too.

Lollipop's head came up again. She tumbled from the bed to the floor and skidded on the buttercream ceramic tiles as she scrambled for the chest. The wooden spoon went out as Lollipop went in, and the lid came down with a resounding slam.

That could mean only one of two things. Either Aunt Karen was pulling into the driveway—which couldn't be because she was never, ever early—or . . .

Lucy crawled to the window again and slid it open this time, letting in a blast of cold air that dried out her nostrils in one sniff. With it came what anyone else would have thought was the beyond-annoying sound of a Chihuahua begging for food.

"Pizza delivery," the voice said.

Lucy settled her elbows on the windowsill. "What kind of toppings?"

"Um . . . applesauce?"

"What?" Lucy said.

A dark ponytail surfaced to the window like a periscope on a submarine.

"Whatever," the Chihuahua voice yelped. "I've been out here for ten hours."

"No, you haven't, Januarie." Lucy watched as a round face came into view, chapped-red and puffing air. "Probably more like ten seconds."

Januarie stood up to her full short-for-an-eight-year-old height and clamped her hands, plump as muffins, on the outside stucco sill. "I have to come in," she said. "I have a you-know-what pizza."

"A message from J.J.?" Lucy said.

"Shhh!" Januarie sprayed the sill, her hands, and the front of Lucy's sweatshirt. "We're supposed to talk in code!"

"'You-know-what' is not 'code,'" Lucy said.

Sophie Series

Meet Sophie LaCroix, a creative soul who's destined to become a great film director someday. But many times, her overactive imagination gets her in trouble!

Sophie's World
Book 1 • Softcover • ISBN 9780310707561

Sophie's Secret
Book 2 • Softcover • ISBN 9780310707578

Sophie and the Scoundrels
Book 3 • Softcover • ISBN 9780310707585

Sophie's Irish Showdown
Book 4 • Softcover • ISBN 9780310707592

Sophie's First Dance?
Book 5 • Softcover • ISBN 9780310707608

Sophie's Stormy Summer
Book 6 • Softcover • ISBN 9780310707615

Sophie Breaks the Code
Book 7 • Softcover • ISBN 9780310710226

Sophie Tracks a Thief
Book 8 • Softcover • ISBN 9780310710233

Sophie Flakes Out
Book 9 • Softcover • ISBN 9780310710240

Sophie Loves Jimmy
Book 10 • Softcover • ISBN 9780310710257

Sophie Loses the Lead
Book 11 • Softcover • ISBN 9780310710264

Sophie's Encore
Book 12 • Softcover • ISBN 9780310710271

Available now at your local bookstore! Visit www.faithgirlz.com

faiThGirLz!
the beauty of believing

Devotions

No Boys Allowed
Devotions for Girls
Softcover • ISBN 9780310707189

This short, ninety-day devotional for girls ages 10 and up is written in an upbeat, lively, funny, and tween-friendly way, incorporating the graphic, fast-moving feel of a teen magazine.

Girlz Rock
Devotions for You
Softcover • ISBN 9780310708995

In this ninety-day devotional, devotions like "Who Am I?" help pave the spiritual walk of life, and the "Girl Talk" feature poses questions that really bring each message home. No matter how bad things get, you can always count on God.

Chick Chat
More Devotions for Girls
Softcover • ISBN 9780310711438

This ninety-day devotional brings the Bible right into your world and offers lots to learn and think about.

Shine On, Girl!
Devotions to Keep You Sparkling
Softcover • ISBN 9780310711445

This ninety-day devotional will "totally" help teen girls connect with God, as well as learn his will for their lives.

Nonfiction

Everybody Tells Me to Be Myself but I Don't Know Who I Am

Softcover • ISBN 9780310712954

This new addition to the Faithgirlz! line helps girls face the challenges of being their true selves with fun activities, interactive text, and insightful tips.

Girl Politics

Softcover • ISBN 9780310712961

Parents and kids alike may think that getting teased or arguing with friends is just part of growing up, but where is the line between normal kid stuff and harmful behavior? This book is a guide for girls on how to deal with girl politics, God-style.

Beauty Lab

Softcover • ISBN 9780310712763

Beauty tips and the secret of true inner beauty are revealed in this interactive, inspirational, fun addition to the Faithgirlz! line.

What's a Girl to Do?

Softcover • ISBN 9780310713487

In this new devotional from Kristi Holl, you'll learn what to do in confusing situations, and also about the kind of person God wants you to be: pretty both inside and out.

Available now at your local bookstore! Visit www.faithgirlz.com

We want to hear from you. Please send your comments about this book to us in care of zreview@zondervan.com. Thank you.

ZONDERVAN.com/
AUTHORTRACKER
follow your favorite authors